Lincoln's Bishop

Lincoln's Bishop

A President,
a Priest,
and the
Fate of 300 Dakota Sioux Warriors

GUSTAV NIEBUHR

HarperOne
An Imprint of HarperCollins*Publishers*

HarperOne

All scripture quotations are from the Authorized (King James) Version.

Photo on p. viii courtesy of the Universal History Archive/UIG/The Bridgeman Art Library. Photo on p. ix courtesy of the Library of Congress, Brady-Hardy Photograph Collection. Photo on p. x courtesy of the Library of Congress. Photo on p. 184 courtesy of the Minnesota Historical Society.

HarperCollins books may be purchased for educational, business, or sales promotional use. For information please e-mail the Special Markets Department at SPsales@harpercollins.com.

HarperCollins website: http://www.harpercollins.com

HarperCollins®, ✦®, and HarperOne™ are trademarks of HarperCollins Publishers.

FIRST EDITION

Library of Congress Cataloging-in-Publication Data

Niebuhr, Gustav.
    Lincoln's bishop : a president, a priest, and the fate of 300 Dakota Sioux warriors / Gustav Niebuhr.
        pages cm
    Includes bibliographical references and index.
    ISBN 978-0-06-209768-2
    1. Dakota Indians—Wars, 1862–1865. 2. Dakota Indians—Government relations—History—19th century. 3. Whipple, Henry Benjamin, 1822–1901. 4. Lincoln, Abraham, 1809–1865—Relations with Dakota Indians. 5. Church work with Indians—Episcopal Church—History—19th century. I. Title.
    E83.86.N54   2014
    323.1197'5243—dc23   2013051296

14 15 16 17 18 RRD(H) 10 9 8 7 6 5 4 3 2 1

To Margaret

Contents

Abraham Lincoln, 1865

Henry Benjamin Whipple, 1859

Little Crow, 1862

Introduction

I FIRST HEARD ABOUT HENRY B. WHIPPLE WHEN I HAP-
pened to be a few miles from his birthplace in Adams, New
York, one early March day, cold even by northern New York
standards. I had come up Interstate 81 to lecture at a community college in Watertown, the last city a driver sees before
crossing the bridge over the Saint Lawrence River into Canada.

To orient me, my host—a newspaper editor deeply invested
in his community—shared a handful of names of local, historic
figures he admired. Whipple was near the top of his list. The
name did not register with me, so he helpfully supplied an epi-
taph: "He was the Episcopal bishop who went to see Lincoln to
try to stop a mass hanging of the Sioux Indians." That sentence
landed with an impact that made me want more information,
and I sought it as soon as I got back to Syracuse University,
where I teach. I pursued the bishop from there. I found that,
yes, Whipple did go to see Lincoln about the Sioux (henceforth
to be called by their own name, the Dakotas), but the visit took
place in a much larger, more impressive context: years of Whipple's advocacy, including several trips and letters to Washington
in which the bishop demanded a sweeping reform of how the
U.S. government treated Native Americans. Whipple acted as a

one-man movement, seeking respect and protection for American Indians to replace the monstrous fraud and injustice to which he saw them subjected.

It took me little time to find in the story a contemporary resonance. I had recently had occasion to reread one of the most powerful Christian documents of my lifetime, Rev. Dr. Martin Luther King Jr.'s "Letter from a Birmingham Jail." It seemed to speak to Whipple's best work, as a dedicated social reformer laboring on behalf of abused people amidst a time of great violence.

King's essay, written principally to white "moderates" during the Civil Rights campaign in 1963, focuses on the paradox of religious figures and institutions that claim moral authority yet do little with it, despite being figuratively sunk to their breastbones in the poisonous waters of injustice. King's prose bore heartbreaking witness. "On sweltering summer days and crisp autumn mornings I have looked at the South's beautiful churches with their lofty spires pointing heavenward. I have beheld the impressive outlines of her massive religious-education buildings. Over and over I have found myself asking: 'What kind of people worship here? Who is their God?'"[1]

Early Christians, he recalled, confronted head-on the Roman Empire's social abuses. Their acts of dangerous defiance contrasted with the largely silent Southern church of his own time, one he said had "a weak, ineffectual voice with an uncertain sound." King's twentieth-century words, read anew, seemed by contrast to lift Bishop Whipple from an obscure past. Few among the oppressors, King said, could understand the yearnings of the oppressed, "and still fewer have the vision to see that injustice must be rooted out by strong, persistent, and determined action."[2]

Whipple does not bear comparison with King. Who does? But he possessed a motivation similar to the vision King commanded. He placed Christianity above race and ethnicity—

specifically focusing on Native Americans—at a time when few whites, clergy or otherwise, did likewise.

That an individual Christian might act as if the requirements of the faith trump racial and cultural divisions is a difficult task, but not an impossible one. Perhaps because something similar had happened within my own extended family, I felt all the more drawn to Whipple. In 1952, my uncle Lansing Hicks, a young Episcopal priest from North Carolina who had married my mother's middle sister, resigned in protest from his position as a professor of theology at a divinity school in Tennessee. It was the job he had always wanted. He had a toddler son, and his wife, my aunt Helen, was pregnant with their second child. But the school's trustees raised a serious moral obstacle when they declined to desegregate the school, which would have allowed African Americans to study there. Lansing, along with seven of his colleagues, rebuked the board, declaring its decision "untenable in the light of Christian ethics." The trustees remained unmoved. My uncle gave up his dream job, resigning along with his seven colleagues.

In the mid-nineteenth century, journalist John O'Sullivan coined the phrase "manifest destiny," shorthand for white Americans' territorial ambitions and the related belief the Indians would vanish before them. As a newly consecrated bishop, Whipple moved to Minnesota in 1859, a year after its political leaders had adopted the idea of manifest destiny on an official state seal, showing a white farmer at his plow watching an Indian ride into the setting sun. Whipple arrived a missionary, eager to preach to Indians and whites alike, but he did not subscribe to a vision of Native American dispossession. That made him a countercultural figure.

A month after Whipple took up residence in the state, he began lobbying on the Indians' behalf, and when he finally reached President Lincoln, he did so at what a less determined individual would have recognized was the worst time possible.

In September 1862 the Dakota War spread death and terror across Minnesota, its principle victims white civilians; the state's leaders demanded Native Americans be exterminated. That did not stop Whipple. He recognized that moral authority, when kept sheathed like a sword in its scabbard, eventually loses its purpose.

Prologue

Waiting for Lincoln

WHEN HE STEPPED ACROSS THE THRESHOLD INTO Abraham Lincoln's White House in September 1862, Henry Whipple had come directly from the war that had thrown his state into upheaval. Minnesota's first Protestant Episcopal Church bishop, Whipple estimated that eight hundred civilians had lost their lives, and many bodies still lay unburied on the prairies and creek banks where they had fallen.[1] He had come to tell Lincoln how this catastrophe had occurred—and, more important, how a future such disaster could be avoided.

By coincidence (or, as some might have it, the hand of providence), the bishop chose an extraordinary moment to approach Lincoln. The very week he went to see the president, more than seventy-five thousand Union troops marched west through Maryland to confront General Robert E. Lee's Army of Northern Virginia, which had crossed the Potomac River in a daring invasion of the North. That Wednesday, the Army of the Potomac, commanded by General George McClellan (whom Whipple counted as a friend), fought Lee outside the village of Sharpsburg, at Antietam Creek. By sunset, more than twenty-two thousand men were dead, wounded, or missing, making that September 17 the bloodiest single day in American history.

Neither side emerged clearly victorious, but McClellan had possession of the battlefield, a tactical win that would stifle talk in
Europe about its governments recognizing the South as an independent nation. In the office in which he would meet Whipple,
Lincoln had quietly drafted an executive order to free nearly
four million men, women, and children held as slaves. He kept
the document in a desk drawer, awaiting a sign from God that
the moment had come to make it public. He would recognize
Antietam as providing that sign.[2]

By then, Whipple had spent three years devoted to a particular cause. It had finally carried him to the portals of civil
power, and he told Lincoln about it in person. Almost since
the moment he became his church's youngest bishop in 1859,
Henry Whipple was convinced that a part of the federal government was brutally, dangerously corrupt and needed a thorough
reform in the name of peace and the nation's standing with
God. His target was the Office of Indian Affairs, a unit of the
Department of the Interior. The men who ran the office had the
primary task of negotiating treaties with the Indian tribes, typically swapping tribal lands for promises to pay an annual sub-
sidy to maintain the peoples who would no longer have access to
their traditional territories, where they had hunted, fished, and
grown crops. The office appointed agents to oversee and inter-
act with the tribes. It also allowed the agents to allot licenses to
businessmen who wanted to trade with the Indians.[3] From what
Whipple had seen in Minnesota, he thought the treaties unfair,
the agents ignorant, and the traders avaricious.

Whipple had worked on his own initiative, steadily building
up a campaign. He had discussed his concerns with Minnesotans, Indian and white alike; sent letters to friends in business
and politics; and even taken his case once before to Washington, DC, seeking to persuade men with power of his point. On
that earlier journey, he had gone, he said, "to plead for justice"[4]
for Native Americans. Increasingly, he regarded their treatment

as a national scandal. But on the earlier trip, he had not attained the White House. This time, he waited to deliver his message to the president.

Lincoln knew the salient facts of the Dakota War, then still convulsing Minnesota. It had begun with an attack against a federal installation in the state's south on August 18. Driven primarily by the Mdewakantons, one of the four Dakota bands in the state, the war spread across rich agricultural land, devastating farms and villages. Lincoln, like Whipple, estimated eight hundred rural men and women killed—a civilian death toll much higher than any single clash brought about by Civil War armies. Earlier in September, acting at the urging of Minnesota's leaders, Lincoln had dispatched a general to direct the counterattacks.[5]

As a wartime president, Lincoln was used to being sought out by clergy members, never a rare species in American public life. Those who claimed they had a special message bearing on national policy, received directly from God, tried his patience. He relieved his irritation with humor. Earlier in September 1862, a delegation of Chicago ministers had called on him with an ecumenical statement demanding he move immediately to emancipate the slaves. "I hope," Lincoln replied, "that it will not be irreverent for me to say that if it is probable that God would reveal his will to others, on a point so connected with my duty, it might be supposed he would directly reveal it to me."[6]

Whipple took a less sweeping and omniscient tack. He stated his goal simply: the Indians must be protected from corrupt government agents and rapacious traders, especially those who dealt in liquor and abused women. He had traveled widely enough among Minnesota's Indians that he could tell stories that riveted audiences and incisively illustrated his argument. "In sight of the mission house, an Indian woman was violated by brutal white men," the bishop recalled in an essay written for fellow Episcopalians, "and then such demon-like cruelty inflicted on her person that she died under their hands. It was in sight of a village of white men; it was made known to the agent. No one was punished and no investigation made."[7] When he arrived in Washington in mid-September, he had a potent illustration to offer Lincoln of what the consequences of federal Indian policy could be: Minnesota was in chaos. Some of the Dakotas, a tribe that had once considered the state's southern half its domain, had been waging a war for four weeks. Whipple personally knew civilians uprooted and sent, terrified, in flight. He was fully aware from conversations he had had that many Minnesotans blamed the violence solely on the Indians. Whipple blamed the government. "Again and again," the bishop wrote, "I had said publicly that as certain as any fact in human history, a nation which sowed robbery would reap a harvest of blood."[8]

Anyone passing by Whipple that day, September 15, would have noticed two striking facts about the man.[9] First was the military eminence of his escort. The bishop came accompanied by General Henry Halleck, a West Point graduate and scholar of arms whom Lincoln had appointed seven weeks earlier as general in chief of all Union forces. (Halleck would shortly prove a disappointment to Lincoln in that position.) The bishop and the general were cousins and had corresponded for years.[10] But Whipple, even though he was a stranger in Washington, would have drawn attention in his own right. At six feet two inches tall—nearly as tall as Lincoln—he had half a foot's height on the average man of the time. He could nearly look Lincoln in the eye. At forty, he was more than a dozen years younger than the president and slimmer. In an era in which many men, including Lincoln, wore facial hair, Whipple kept himself clean-shaven. He swept his dark hair back and let it grow long down his neck, in a style some of his Indian acquaintances recognized favorably.

That day in the White House, Whipple's appearance would have included a discordant note. He had a bandaged hand, the result of an injury two weeks earlier. He had hurt it while sewing up wounds suffered by white settlers in flight from the Dakotas.[11] The bishop had spent days serving as a nurse in a makeshift hospital he had organized not far from the fighting. At some point, his needle had slipped, and the hand had become painfully infected.

Nothing in Whipple's biography before his becoming a bishop indicated that he would summon the commitment to attempt such a project as a wholesale change in federal government attitudes toward Native Americans. Nothing, that is, unless one counts the latent effect on him of two people from his early childhood: his mother, Elizabeth Wager Whipple, and an elderly Revolutionary War veteran named Peter Doxtater, who as a child had been taken captive by Indians.

Two years before Whipple's birth on February 15, 1822, his parents settled in Adams, New York, a small town lying astride a commercial track connecting the Erie Canal with Ontario, Canada. His father, John, established himself as a merchant, with a general store that catered to farmers. John's letters to Henry, written when Henry was an adolescent at boarding school, display a tender regard for his oldest son's welfare and happiness. The elder Whipple, who signed himself "your affectionate father," sent his son occasional small gifts of money and took care to warn him away from "groceries," businesses that sold liquor.[12] Elizabeth Whipple made a deeper impression. She instilled in her son the belief that he should take the side of the injured and oppressed. He would find God there. Whipple, as an old man nearing death, would recall her words to him as a child: "Never hesitate to defend the weak." She imparted to her son a lasting commitment to social justice. Were Henry to see someone abused, mocked, or otherwise cruelly treated, he ought to step in. So effective was her message that Whipple recalled it twice in the first five pages of his autobiography.[13]

The bishop left little on paper about the other formative influence in his childhood, the man who effectively became his moral tutor on the subject of American Indians. Henry, aged seven or eight, met Peter Doxtater, aged eighty, when the latter was still vigorous and gifted with an ability to relate stories of personal adventure. The stories made Doxtater's household a magnet for Adams boys. The old man, speaking to a young audience gathered at his hearth, played a role as the operator of a time machine, his stories opening a door to a distant past.

Doxtater, whose farmhouse crowned a short, steep hill, was a singular presence in Adams. Born into a Palatine German community in the Mohawk River Valley, Doxtater had served in the Continental army against the British and had fought in the Battle of Oriskany, in 1777, near present-day Rome, New York. One of the fiercest engagements of the Revolution, it began with the American forces ambushed—together with their Oneida Indian allies—and ended in their triumph, thwarting a British plan to divide New York militarily.[14] In 1800, he had moved with his family to Adams, securing the town's first property deed.[15] He was known among his neighbors for not only his service in the American Revolution but also his memories of an earlier conflict, the French and Indian War, which had ravaged the New York frontier. His stories from that earlier conflict entranced Whipple.

In 1757, at about age seven, Peter Doxtater had been taken captive, along with his siblings, by Indians during a raid. A mixed party of French and Indian soldiers had targeted Doxtater's village, a Mohawk River settlement called German Flatts, then part of the western salient of white settlement in New York.[16] The Doxtater children were taken to Canada and adopted into a new community and its culture. They lived among Indian families, learned a new language, and absorbed lessons about hunting and fishing. They were told stories of the cosmos they would not otherwise have heard. Doxtater forgot most of his English.[17] He became an Indian.

In his autobiography, the bishop wrote with pointed brevity about his friend. "In my native town there was an old man who had been captured by the Indians when a child and had lived many years with them. I delighted in listening to his stories of Indian life, and insensibly my heart was touched and prepared for the love which I was to feel for this poor people." The importance of the recollection lies in the phrase "my heart was touched and prepared."[18] That speaks, decades afterward, of transformation. The stories Whipple heard about Indians, from a man who had known and lived with them, prepared the future bishop to weather the criticism and hostility he would encounter from whites in frontier Minnesota who had much less interest in Native Americans than he did. Doxtater's stories carried a moral impact. When relating the experiences of his captivity among the Indians, Doxtater conveyed an unexpected message: he and his siblings had been treated kindly. The former captive told about being adopted into a tribe that cared for him as one of their own. Had Doxtater been treated differently or had a far less adventurous personality, he might have chosen to remember his boyhood experiences negatively, as a long and frightening exile in a foreign land. Such a message likely would not have produced a positive effect on those who heard it. Instead, Doxtater recalled a fascination with the new world into which he found himself inducted.

The brief accounts of Doxtater's captivity, recorded by neighbors after his death and preserved in Adams, regularly include references to his having been treated well.[19] That could only have come from him; its repetition suggests he emphasized it. He would have known neighbors killed in the raid on German Flatts; he would have heard their screams. He had an experience of being ripped from home and parents. When he returned, in the 1760s, after British soldiers came upon him and his siblings and paid a ransom to take them back to New York State, he heard how his mother, beside herself with sorrow and anxiety after the raid, had pulled on her fingers until they popped, dislocated from their sockets.[20] She had no idea her children had survived. Nothing would have stopped him, then, from telling a different kind of story to children like Henry Whipple much later. Yet Peter Doxtater, as an adult, chose to focus instead on his life among the Indians as exciting, rich, and meaningful. That helped shape Whipple's consciousness. A former frontiersman, sharing stories from his childhood, prepared Whipple for his vocation on the frontier—and for a mission to the White House more than a century after that raid in the Mohawk Valley.

At their best, good stories have the power to uplift and educate. They can shape the moral imagination. They can nurture an inclination toward honesty, compassion, justice. They can inspire a child to become the kind of man or woman who recognizes wrongdoing and believes he or she has an imperative— and the ability—to act against it. Such stories can foster a moral self-confidence in those who hear and remember them.

"In my boyhood," Whipple wrote, looking back from a distance of six decades, "I used to visit an aged man by the name of Peter Doxtater who was a soldier in the Revolutionary War. In his childhood, he was captured by the Algonquin Indians and adopted into the tribe. . . . It was the delight of the boys of the village to sit at the old man's feet and listen to his thrilling stories of Indian life, hunting, and warfare." Whipple added, crucially, "I have never doubted that this with the lessons of my mother, who taught me to take the part of the weak and helpless, was the foundation of my first interest in the North American Indians."[21] Whipple could not have put it more plainly and succinctly. The statement is crucial to understanding him.

At age eleven Whipple was sent by his parents to Presbyterian boarding schools in the Erie Canal cities of Oneida and Rome. The details of his life from his adolescence to his decision to settle in Chicago at age thirty-five are varied but lack the drama of the life that followed. Whipple spent a year studying at the Oberlin Collegiate Institute in Ohio. Oberlin had a notorious reputation among many, both Northerners and Southerners, while it was also admired by a relative few, for its close association with abolitionism, the most radical wing of the emerging antislavery movement. Abolitionists argued for the immediate freedom of African American slaves. Within a few years of its founding in 1833, Oberlin began admitting blacks and women as students. That Whipple's parents should send him there reflected, at least in part, a close family connection to the college. John Whipple's brother George, a Presbyterian minister and an ardent abolitionist, taught mathematics at Oberlin and would devote years of his life to antislavery work and African American education.[22] After his time at Oberlin, Henry Whipple declared he hated slavery, but he did not call himself an abolitionist. In a diary he kept on a long journey he took through the South in 1843–44, he wrote that he saw slavery's end as anything but occurring soon. To be freed, the slaves would have to be educated, their owners likely compensated for the loss of their labor. Whipple also wrote that he despised slave auctions (he felt they broke up families), but he accepted the myth not uncommon among Northerners that the ranks of slave owners contained many "generous masters."[23] Whipple's uneven thinking on this subject made the clarity of his dedication to the cause of Native Americans' protection all the more notable.

Whipple might have stayed longer at Oberlin if he had not fallen ill at the end of his first year with an unspecified throat ailment, which would recur throughout his life. A doctor recommended he give up academics entirely and begin a more active life, advice that Whipple took seriously enough to return to Adams and join his father in business.[24]

The return to Adams led to another change: within two years, Whipple married Cornelia Wright, the daughter of a prominent local lawyer. Cornelia was a graduate of Emma Willard's school in Troy, New York, and had the equivalent of a college education, which her husband lacked. The bride was also a committed Episcopalian and six years older than Whipple. She had spent some of her early adult years as a tutor in the South, using her money to support a brother's work as a missionary. By 1846, Whipple had parted with the Presbyterianism of his childhood, been baptized and confirmed as an Episcopalian, and begun studying (under the direction of western New York's bishop) for the priesthood.

His first parish was Rome, a familiar place, where he had spent part of his adolescence in boarding school. Whipple spent nearly a decade there. He might well have served longer had not a man named Albert Neely arrived from Chicago. Neely was searching for an energetic young priest who could be tempted by an opportunity to build up a new parish from scratch, primarily among railroad workers.[25] The church in this new parish was the missionary project of wealthy Episcopalians who had spent a year seeking just the right man for the job: an indefatigable worker skilled at fund-raising, uninterested in divisive church politics, and prepared to immerse himself in a new culture with its own specialized language. Neely decided he had found their man in Whipple and offered him $2,000 a year, roughly double what Whipple's parish in Rome paid.

In 1857, Whipple became rector of the Free Church of the Holy Communion, located in rented space in a commodious downtown Chicago building called Metropolitan Hall. (By "free," the church's organizers meant no one who came would have to rent a pew, a common practice in those days.) Whipple worked the rail yards, the bars, and the local businesses in search of prospective members. "I visited every shop, saloon, and factory within a mile of the hall, leaving a card giving the place and hour of worship and stating that I would be at the service of anyone needing help, day or night." He recorded making as many as twenty pastoral calls a day.[26] And he kept an eye out for people in physical need. Should any prospective member of the church be injured in an accident, he said, "I will gladly go to you." Locomotives of the era often lacked reliable brakes. When he heard of a rail-yard accident, Whipple wrote, "I immediately went to the sufferer."[27]

In Chicago, Whipple also formed friendships with men in the upper echelons of railroad management, influential in business and politics. This group included George McClellan. After the Civil War erupted, McClellan traded a railroad executive's business attire for a Union general's uniform. By 1862, he commanded the Army of the Potomac. Another railroad friend, William McAlpine, took Whipple in 1860 to meet Stephen Douglas, then Illinois's Democratic senator and a man of immense political power in the Midwest.

Whipple enjoyed the challenge his Chicago work offered. His name traveled through church circles further than he realized. In the early summer of 1859, he came under the favorable scrutiny of Episcopalians who were preparing to meet four hundred miles northwest in Minnesota. These men were eager to elect a bishop to supervise and expand church work in the new state. Episcopalians within a diocese—a regional church jurisdiction comprising a state or part of a state—choose their bishop during a convention, priests and lay delegates making up two separate groups that each cast their own ballots. To complete the process, a majority of both houses must agree on a single candidate. On June 29 of that year, two dozen men gathered in Saint Paul, Minnesota's capital, and on their third ballot elected Whipple to be the state's first Episcopal bishop.

Whipple had not sought the office, nor had anyone told him his name would be entered in the balloting. His election resulted from a deadlock. The little convention took two votes by secret ballot and failed to reach a majority on any candidate. Both times, however, one person put in Whipple's name. After the group had adjourned for prayer, someone asked, just who was Henry Whipple? A local priest resolved the mystery, citing Whipple's work in Chicago and the positive impression it had made. A missionary priest in Chicago could become a missionary bishop in Minnesota. Whipple then received a crucial endorsement from a layman at the convention. Napoleon Dana, a West Point graduate and banker, said he had met Whipple and thought he showed "a peculiar fitness for pioneer work and for work among the laboring classes." Dana's recommendation carried the day. Now all that was needed was for someone to tell Whipple.[28]

Whipple had to think over the offer. He caught a train back to Adams, apparently to seek his parents' counsel. For an ambitious priest in fast-growing Chicago, becoming bishop of Minnesota did not represent a clear step up—at least not in secular terms. It meant saying good-bye to a cosmopolitan hub and setting off for a raw, lightly settled state with vast horizons. Minnesota's Episcopalians numbered fewer than five hundred, and they were widely scattered. Also, the men who had elected Whipple bishop set his salary at $1,500 a year—a 25 percent pay cut from what he had been earning in Chicago. They could not offer him housing, either, as Minnesota had no previous resident bishop. It took Whipple nearly two weeks to decide, but he said yes.

By mid-winter of 1860 Whipple had a residence in the southwestern Minnesota town of Faribault where he settled Cornelia and their six children. He also acquired a horse and wagon, and set off on a pastoral life of exceptional rigor. He calculated that his visitations amounted to three thousand miles of annual travel. More than once he got lost in blizzards, northern plains storms legendary for their ability to freeze hapless travelers and bury them in snow. Whipple credited his horse, Bashaw, with his survival. He came to love the animal and said it had the plain sense and understanding of direction to get them to shelter in remote cabins in times of emergency, saving both their lives.[29]

Very early on, Bishop Whipple made a friend among his scattered flock who became nearly as important to him as his mother and Peter Doxtater had been. Whites knew the man as John Johnson, but Whipple called him by his Indian name: Enmegahbowh, which translates from the Ojibwe language as He Who Prays for His People While Standing. When Whipple stepped onto the streets of Saint Paul as bishop in November 1859, one of the first people he shook hands with was this sturdy, broadshouldered man. The only son of an Ottawa chief, Enmegahbowh was by then about fifty-five years old. A few months earlier, he had been ordained as a deacon in the Episcopal Church, the first Native American to hold that status. Crucially, he made sure that Whipple's first official impressions of Minnesota were not confined to parishes of white settlers. He invited the bishop to undertake an early winter trip with him to visit a mission church called Saint Columba, which catered to the Ojibwes, who lived in the state's north. Enmegahbowh possessed a physical stamina and moral certainty well suited to a frontier missionary. Years earlier he had been a Methodist, but a story circulated that he ran into trouble with his Methodist church after he knocked down a white man who had insulted Enmegahbowh's wife, a baptized Christian known by her English name, Charlotte.[30]

Whipple emerged from the journey north impressed by Indian missions but deeply distressed at the negative effects of white culture on native people. When he met Ojibwes at the mission church, the bishop delighted in hearing the words of the Anglican liturgy in a Native American tongue. Never, he said, had the service "sounded sweeter." But he also became aware of the desperate economy that had developed in the region. The Indians were indebted to traders for goods they purchased and they were highly susceptible to the whiskey those men provided. Its consumption could provoke mayhem to the point of encouraging killing. "This first visit," Whipple said, "was a fearful revelation of the cup of degradation and sorrow which we had pressed to the lips of those Red men." As Whipple drew near Saint Columba, he encountered a *danse macabre* of the plague alcohol had visited on the native population. He passed the body of an Indian murdered by another man in an inebriated rage. He saw hunger, a woman scraping furiously to get at a pine tree's inner bark to obtain nourishment for her near-starving children.[31] The degradation indicated that the Indians were being dealt with very poorly by the state's whites—people who looked like him. He felt God had laid a special responsibility on him. In return, he made a promise, which he later repeated to an assistant, who wrote it down. "The Bishop resolved, God being his helper that he would never turn his back on the heathen[32] whom God had placed at his door."[33] No one—Whipple included—could know the intellectual, emotional, and physical efforts that his vow would demand.

One

The Sunday Afternoon Murders

VIOLENCE CAN ERUPT WITH SLIGHT PROVOCATION; how it happens depends on the temperaments and circumstances of the people involved. An aggressor may unleash irreparable damage after a misunderstanding that, in hindsight, appears surprisingly trivial. Even greater violence may follow such an incident, to the astonishment of onlookers and the agony of those who discover themselves sucked into the whirlwind. Every war, insurrection, or riot has a flash point. The underlying tensions and broad grievances that feed the initial act may be obvious beforehand—or they may not—but some people grasp the root causes of violence and incorporate them into a longer narrative. At that point, too, the first incident is set in a historic context, no longer appearing to be an isolated event. Instead, it takes on a symbolic importance as the rumble of an approaching cataclysm whose destructive power surpasses the imagination of even those who see it erupt.

The Dakota War of 1862 occurred after four young Native American men gunned down five white settlers, one of them an adolescent girl they shot as she stood in a doorway. The perpetrators, members of a recent hunting party, opened fire without warning. The action began and ended in minutes. The manner of their deed did not suggest a clear plan, other than killing. They gained nothing materially; no evidence ever emerged that they had intended to commit robbery. The only explanation ever put forward for why the young men acted when and where they did was this: An hour or so earlier, two of the men had argued over who had the right to a clutch of eggs they had found on the prairie. Could one man among them legitimately raid the hen's nest, as he claimed, or was that nest off-limits, the property of a white settler, as the man's companion asserted? The men (and the other two with them) were famished and tired, so it should have been no surprise that a verbal shoving match erupted between them over the issue. But their argument quickly ratcheted up and the word "coward" got thrown around. Then one of them followed with a careless and lethal dare: If you are so brave, would you kill a white man?[1]

The murders took place in the heat of a summer Sunday, in a lightly peopled stretch of central Minnesota, where the prairies sweep up from the south to meet a dense belt of forest called the Big Woods. By coincidence, it happened to be the same day Bishop Whipple emerged from what he described as a delightfully peaceful and spiritually satisfying visit with Ojibwe Indians in northern Minnesota. He had celebrated Communion with them. Notably among his possessions, he carried a copy of a letter he had written to President Lincoln. In it, Whipple succinctly laid out a program for reforming the federal government's Office of Indian Affairs to better protect all Native Americans, including the Dakotas. The letter, which Whipple had sent earlier in the year, marked the start of a formal relationship between the bishop and his president, one that would lead the bishop to the White House. "When I came to Minnesota, I was startled by the degradation at my door," Whipple had written to Lincoln.[2] A few days earlier in August, when Whipple had reached the Ojibwes, he had read the letter aloud to a chief with whom he had met. Now, on a return path that largely followed the Mississippi River, the bishop learned about "a party of Sioux" hunting in the woods, barely thirty miles from where he drove his wagon. But he would later confess that he knew nothing more than this slim report.[3] So, he passed by the scene of the killing, a couple dozen miles distant.

The hunting party included about twenty men, Dakota Indians from villages on the Minnesota River, which cuts across the state's south before it turns north to join the Mississippi near present-day Minneapolis and Saint Paul. The hunters had come north a week earlier to search the forest for game. Their guns ready, they sought the deer that had once lived abundantly in the woods and had sustained Dakota families for generations. Competition from white settlers had thinned out a once-ample herd. The hunters came up empty, their excursion a disappointment. Fifty or so miles from home, they reached the tiny settlement of Acton on a well-worn track, the Pembina-Henderson Trail, which linked southern Minnesota with Canada. Even the youngest among them could remember a time before game had become so diminished.[4]

The hunters represented a new phenomenon in Dakota life: dispossession. A decade earlier, leaders of the Santee Dakotas (the collective name for four large bands) had gambled on a massive swap: their lands in return for an annual payment from the U.S. Treasury with which, a prominent government agent had assured them, they could happily sustain themselves. The federal government promised in an 1851 treaty to pay the Dakotas a sum of money—in gold—each June. With the annuity, Dakota families were to buy food and clothing, and receive whatever else—such as schools and farming implements—they might need to wean themselves from a traditional hunting economy. The men who had signed the treaty surrendered nearly all Dakota lands within Minnesota, a swathe of territory breathtaking in its vastness, nearly twenty-four million acres. Now, the hunters who gathered near Acton could be counted as

de facto visitors on their historic lands. They could legally claim
nothing but what the treaty, and another that followed in 1857,
had left them: a strip of land, ten miles wide and a hundred
miles long, fronting the Minnesota River's southern bank.

The hunters passed by the cabins, farms, and gardens that
had started to appear in Acton, Forest City, and other settlements in surrounding Meeker County. None of the men were
predisposed to dislike the whites, who had arrived in the past
five or so years. For at least two centuries Dakotas, from in-
fancy, had recognized as their enemy the Ojibwes, the tribe
that claimed the northern and central reaches of Minnesota.
(The new state's name derived directly from a Dakota phrase,
meaning "sky clouded water.") Two centuries earlier, French
missionaries and explorers, ranging south from Canada, had encountered the two tribes and noted their enmity. Dakotas and
Ojibwes fought one another continuously. The Ojibwes (also
known among whites as the Chippewas) forced the Dakotas
out of Wisconsin and northern Minnesota, pushing them south
onto the prairies and lands around the Mississippi River, below
a cascade at present-day Minneapolis that whites called Saint
Anthony Falls. Even as late as the early 1860s, the tribes still
clashed. The very day of the killings, August 17, one member of
the Dakota hunting party boasted that he had proven his bravery in war parties against Ojibwe fighters.[5]

Whites tended to call the Dakotas "the Sioux," a name
originating with the Ojibwes, who had tagged their enemies as
Naduwessi, meaning "little snakes." French explorers adopted a
version of that word, calling the Dakotas *Naduwessioux*, adding
a Gallic plural, later shortened to *Sioux*. It sounded nothing
like *Dakota*, which, by contrast, means "friends." As one early
historian wrote, the root of *Dakota* can mean "society, association, republic."[6] The Dakotas numbered seven substantial
bands, who together hunted across a thousand miles of land,
from the Mississippi River to the northern High Plains. Four of

the bands, collectively the Santee Dakotas, lived in Minnesota.

That morning, the twenty or so men in the hunting party broke up, reorganizing themselves into at least three groups to go their separate ways. A chief wanted to visit a nearby white settlement, Forest City, to reclaim a wagon he had left in pawn. He took some men to help him.[7] A dozen others turned south but stayed nearby. That left the four young men among whom trouble soon began.

All four either lived in or had a connection to Rice Creek Village, a settlement on the Dakota reservation. The village stood near a federal outpost, the Lower Sioux Agency, a clutch of administrative buildings and trading centers occupying a bluff above the Minnesota River. Despite its proximity to federal oversight, Rice Creek Village had a reputation among other Dakotas and whites as a place that attracted young and often discontented men.[8] This included Dakotas who resented the results of the treaties the Santee bands had signed with the government at two sites, Traverse des Sioux and Mendota. Before the agreements took place in the summer of 1851, the Dakotas had been lords of the land throughout southern and central Minnesota, west of the Mississippi. Leading whites in the region had coveted this land as they might a new Eden. Alexander Ramsey, a former congressman from Pennsylvania who had moved west and risen to prominence in Minnesota, appointed as its first territorial governor, had been instrumental in pressing the Dakotas to cede their land. Ramsey described the territory with the enthusiasm of a dedicated real estate salesman hunting up buyers. The future state, he declared, was "rich and salubrious . . . equal in soil to any portion of the valley of the Mississippi; and in healthfulness, is probably superior to any part of the American Continent."[9] By 1862, Ramsey had been elected governor of the state.

Had the four Dakota men not committed murder in August 1862, they might well have lived out their lives anonymous to all but their friends and families. Instead, they gained a unique place in the story of a war that shattered the state, at the very time when the United States descended into the far bloodier depths of the Civil War, as the escalating battles between North and South consumed soldiers by the thousands. The four men who reached Acton were known as Brown Wing, Breaking Up, Killing Ghost, and Runs Against Something When Crawling. Years later, a chief named Jerome Big Eagle identified the quartet and described the argument that had broken out between two of them. One man had found a bird's nest on the ground near a fence and scooped out four eggs. He might have eaten them there—or, more likely, shared them—had not one of his companions challenged him, declaring that the nest belonged to nearby whites and, if the eggs were taken, trouble might follow. Incensed, the man with the eggs smashed them to the ground. His companion mocked him for putting on a display of phony boldness. The first man accused the other of being afraid of whites. "You are a coward," he said, as Big Eagle told it. "Yes, you are afraid of the white man. You are afraid to take even an egg from him, though you are half-starved." The argument rattled on, the men's anger increasing. At some point, one raised the stakes, daring his companion to show his courage by killing a white man. The violence that followed stemmed from opportunity, Big Eagle said.[10] It happened pointlessly, random blood spilled upon the prairie.

As they quarreled, Brown Wing and his three companions came upon Robinson Jones's homestead. They turned into his yard. Jones had lived in Acton for five years, having migrated south from a lumber camp and staked a claim near a friend, Howard Baker. Jones had married Baker's mother. The couple had adopted two children, a girl, aged fifteen that summer, and a much younger boy. Both had been orphaned through a relative's death. In 1861, Jones became Acton's postmaster, his cabin serving as post office. He and his wife also served food there and sold drink—whiskey. They kept glasses on display, and bottles too. Whites who despised Indians on principle later claimed the Dakota men demanded Jones give them the drink, but others who closely investigated the incident emphatically declared the men neither asked for nor took the liquor.[11]

Jones cut a formidable figure. As a former lumberjack, he was muscular and carried himself with a ramrod posture, as if he were a military officer. He stood just above six feet tall. By one account, Jones could also seem brusque, at least with the Dakotas. He happened to be home with the children when the four men came knocking. The Indians made an unusual sight, a picture of a native culture in transition under the influence of a growing white invasion of their lands. Two of the Dakota men wore coats cut and sewn like those of the white settlers. Jones recognized his visitors as men he had seen hunting in the area before, but he turned them down when they asked him for food, telling them only his wife—then away from the cabin—did the cooking. By one account, he also challenged one of the men, saying he had lent the man a shotgun several months previously and had never seen it again.[12]

Given the immediate circumstances, entering into an argument with four armed and hungry men would appear foolish. The encounter would violate the Dakotas' idea of good manners. As Bishop Whipple would write, hospitality was "sacred" among the Indians he met in Minnesota. "Their wigwams are open, and they have an unwritten law that any one has a right to sleep in them. Permission is never asked, but when a stranger enters it is accepted as a matter of course, nothing being said on either side."[13]

White settlers had little cause to fear the Dakotas, even if some of them looked on Indians with frank contempt as racial inferiors. The bands in Minnesota held no reputation for aggression against whites. In the seventeenth century, Rev. Jacques Marquette, a Jesuit explorer of the upper Midwest, paid the

Dakotas a compliment, comparing the tribe to the Iroquois in New York, a formidable native alliance, and saying they inclined toward peace and "never attack till attacked."[14] He credited them as honest dealers. For two centuries, whites who met them generally considered the Dakotas friendly and humane. That may help explain the uproar of surprise and anger that followed an outbreak of violence in 1857, when a relative handful of Indians, following a dissident chief named Inkpaduta, raided white settlements in northern Iowa. It took place during a harsh winter, when Dakota food reserves had run perilously low. Inkpaduta's men invaded cabins built by settlers near Spirit Lake, across the border in Iowa. Thirty-eight people died in the raid. On the frontier, settlers reacted with terror. Then events took a peculiar turn. Local government officials—unable to mount an effective infantry pursuit through the snow—coerced a chief named Little Crow, from the Dakotas' Mdewakanton band, to pursue the renegades. The officials threatened to cut off the Dakotas' annuity payments unless they took the lead in punishing Inkpaduta. Little Crow acceded and, with some handpicked Dakota soldiers, chased after the marauders for two weeks, eventually surprising them and killing three. Little Crow returned to little thanks. A year later he went to Washington, DC, with a party of Dakota chiefs to negotiate another treaty, but once there, he could not persuade the commissioner of Indian affairs that, by defending whites from an enemy, he and his own band should be treated with greater respect by the government amidst the negotiations.[15]

Jones, after rebuffing his visitors' request for food, left his home and children and took a path to the Bakers' cabin, where his wife had gone that morning. The Dakota men followed. At the Bakers' home, they found six adults. One couple, Viranus and Rosa Ann Webster, had arrived from Michigan in a covered wagon. The Indians asked for and received water. So too did two other Dakota men—members of the original hunting party—who stopped by the property and shortly left. Baker's wife later recalled that all the Dakotas they met that afternoon seemed friendly. She thought that, once the two visitors departed, the other four would go too. But they did not.

What happened next remains clouded by the ensuing violence. Isaac Heard, an attorney closely involved in the military trials after this war, said Jones again brought up the matter of his missing gun; the Indians denied taking it. One of the four Dakota men suggested a shooting contest with the settlers, to see who might be best at hitting a mark some distance away. The contest went but a single round. The Indians fired. And so did Jones and Baker.[16] The Dakotas reloaded. Jones and Baker did not. And, then, suddenly, one of the four turned his gun on Viranus Webster, standing nearby and looking on. Another man fired at Baker, emptying one shotgun barrel, then the other. A bullet struck Jones's wife as she rushed toward the door of the Bakers' cabin. Jones was shot last. Baker's wife later said he fell wounded near the Websters' wagon.

With that, the action ceased. The other two women were unhurt in the mêlée. The volley of gunfire echoed out across the prairie. Members of the hunting party heard it and worried that the whites in Acton had set upon their friends. Clara Wilson, the Jones's adopted daughter must have heard the shots too. Standing in her cabin's doorway as the four assailants departed, she became their fifth victim. In a final destructive act, one man fired a bullet that caught her squarely in the upper body. She bled to death on the cabin floor. The four men then went to a neighbor's property and took two horses, one each for two men to ride. They took nothing else.[17]

Jones did not die quickly. The two surviving women retained enough composure, after the Indians left, to slip a pillow under his head. It did little to ease his pain. Lying prone upon the ground, he pounded his boot heels into the dirt and tore up clumps of grass with his hands. Once death took him, the two women hurried several miles to a neighbor's house. The neighbor, in turn, sent a boy to a settlement called Ripley, where local men had called a meeting to find recruits for the Northern armies in the Civil War. As Isaac Heard wrote in his account of the Dakota War, "So incredulous were the people of any hostility on the part of the Indians, that they did not credit what the boy said for some little time."[18] Then they sent a plea to Forest City for armed help.

It might have ended there, had the four men found a way to disappear, heading west toward the plains. Instead, Brown Wing and his three companions reached Rice Creek Village before sundown, riding stolen horses, and shared their story with a village headman named Red Middle Voice. He in turn took it to another nearby chief, Shakopee, who presided over a larger village. In a council held there, a consensus emerged that the situation demanded they take the matter to a more prominent leader, Little Crow, the chief who four years earlier had been denied greater respect by the commissioner of Indian affairs in Washington. On August 17, 1862, just hours after the murders in Acton, Brown Wing and his companions paid Little Crow a call, demanding he join them in a general war on whites.

Later that Sunday, whites in Meeker County, investigating reports of the shootings, confirmed the murders. The next morning, a local judge conducted an inquest on the Baker property, with testimony from the surviving women. Dozens of settlers gathered to watch the proceedings. In an ironic note, several Dakotas who belonged to the original hunting party turned up within sight of the gathering. They had gone searching for their four friends. Spotted by settlers who took them either for the murderers or their sympathizers, the Dakotas fled the scene ahead of armed pursuers.[19]

By then, war had already exploded fifty miles to the south along the Minnesota River Valley, where the federal government maintained the Lower Sioux Agency. Billowing clouds of smoke rose from the agency's burning buildings. The bodies of men and women caught by surprise lay scattered across the grounds. Almost from the moment that Red Middle Voice and Shakopee had led a group of Dakota men through the night to see Little Crow, a debate of life-and-death proportions had shaken the chief's house. Shortly before sunrise, the issue was resolved, with the advocates of war winning out. For the next five weeks, until state militia upset a cleverly planned Dakota ambush at Wood Lake, southern Minnesota would feel the wounding terror of dozens of acts of violence. Some destroyed entire settlements.

News traveled slowly on the frontier, by word of mouth from outlying settlements. Among the white population, no one in any real position of authority heard about the murders for another day or two. Bishop Whipple, driving his wagon south on August 17, reached Saint Cloud, a Mississippi River city, on his way to the capital, Saint Paul. He had every reason to feel refreshed. He had spent nearly two weeks traveling among the Ojibwes. Those with whom he had met had received him warmly, and he had imbibed deeply of the outdoors, journeying by canoe and on foot. The natural world impressed the forty-year-old bishop, an ardent fisherman who could awake from a night's sleep outdoors with a prayer on his lips. He thanked God for the beauty around him. He took satisfaction in being able to share with the Ojibwes a glimmer of the political success he had worked hard to achieve. After all, he had with him that copy of the letter he had written to Lincoln, and he had told the Ojibwes that the president had acknowledged it.

But Whipple's summer had also been one of considerable anxiety. Before he had traveled to Ojibwe country, he had journeyed to the Dakotas, a pastoral visit that had filled him with foreboding. To be sure, there had been spiritual rewards. Visiting the four Dakota bands living on their narrow reservation along the Minnesota River, the bishop had preached, baptized, and even laid a cornerstone for a church. He had talked with Rev. Samuel Hinman, a young missionary he had appointed two years previously to serve the tribe. He had also found many of the Dakotas to be unsettled and angry.[20]

Whipple's call on the Dakotas coincided with signs of a growing crisis on the reservation. He had arrived in late June, typically the time when the government sent its annuity payment. (Henry David Thoreau, the great naturalist, had visited the reservation the previous June, in time to see the gold delivered and to gain a clear sense that the Indians "were quite dissatisfied with the white man's treatment of them."[21]) But in June 1862, the gold had not arrived, nor did anyone claim certain knowledge of why it had not. Indians gathering at the two federal installations on the reservation—the Upper and Lower Sioux agencies—received no explanation for the delay. Many were already hungry. The result was an unhappy excitement that the bishop found unsettling. "I had never seen the Indians looking so restless," he wrote. The sense of grievance extended the length of the narrow reservation along the Minnesota River. At the Upper Sioux Agency, the two Dakota bands living furthest west, the Sissetons and Wahpekons, appeared "most turbulent," in Whipple's estimation. But worse lay to the southeast, around the Lower Sioux Agency. To his great unease, he found the Mdewakanton men, whose villages lay near the agency, engaging in traditional dances that Whipple took as a sign of their agitation. "Every day some heathen dance took place," he said, "a monkey dance, a begging dance, or a scalp dance." The bishop, who had been visiting the reservation since 1860, also found himself on the receiving end of social snubs, a development out of keeping with the respect he had previously offered and received. "Occasionally one of the men would refuse to shake hands with me. I knew what it meant, that he wanted to boast that he would not take the hand of a white man, which was always a danger signal."[22]

That summer, young men on the reservation established a "soldiers' lodge," a sort of political club that allowed them to meet secretly for discussions, without advice or intervention from older men.[23] White traders who watched the situation develop worried openly about it. In the absence of the annuity payment, many Indians lacked cash to buy staples. Waiting, encamped near the agencies, meant they were not out hunting, which worsened the situation. In the absence of real news from Washington that could explain the delay, rumors began to take hold. Whipple learned to his astonishment that a clerk in one of the stores had told the Indians to forget about the money, that the government would not send it. Equally distressing, the man had told the Indians that his store would extend no further credit to the Dakotas until they could pay in cash—which, of course, they could not without their money.[24] In making these statements, the clerk had directly contradicted the local Indian agent, Thomas Galbraith, who had been trying to reassure the Dakotas that the money would come through. What trust existed between the Dakotas and the government agents appeared to be breaking down. (In a sad irony, the long-delayed annuity payment finally arrived in Minnesota, but that news came only after the war had begun.)

As background to the tensions among the Dakotas lay the larger issue of the Civil War, an unavoidable subject even on Minnesota's frontier. Since the fall of Fort Sumter in Charleston Harbor, South Carolina, fourteen months earlier, much had gone wrong for the North. Union armies found themselves outfought and outgeneraled by their Southern counterparts. None of that was a secret. The bishop also learned that the Dakotas had become keenly aware that Washington needed soldiers and competent commanders. Men recruited off the Minnesota frontier depleted the number of soldiers staffing its forts—among them, Fort Ridgely, emplaced on the Minnesota River's north side to maintain federal authority over the reservation's lower section. In the traders' stores, periodicals like *Harper's Weekly* and *Frank Leslie's Illustrated Newspaper* chronicled massive battles, with artists' drawings to lend visual drama. The Dakotas paid close attention to the war's progress, Whipple noticed. "The pictorial papers containing Civil War scenes, which the traders kept on their counters, deeply interested the Indians, who plied questions about the battles and their results." He added, "Up to this time, August 1862, the Union troops had been defeated."[25] To younger Dakotas, it might have appeared then that Minnesota, with many of her young men fighting hundreds of miles away, lay open to be reclaimed. Hunting lands surrendered in two flawed treaties could be regained, farmers and townspeople killed or driven away.

Whipple, although anxious, did not allow the turbulence to interfere with his plans for developing the Episcopal Church on the reservation. He had dedicated himself to building up a mission there as soon as he set foot among the Dakotas. He had established a church, named after Saint John, assigned Hinman as its missionary, and gathered a small congregation of Indians. In July 1862, despite the sense of unrest around him, Whipple laid the cornerstone for a permanent building for Saint John. He had, after all, worked at growing the Episcopal Church, making it a more visible presence, since his first posting as a parish priest in Rome, New York. Most important for the Dakota mission, he had developed friendships with individual Indians. These men and women would render invaluable humanitarian assistance during the coming war. Although worried by what he experienced, Whipple had no knowledge a war would be so soon in coming. But he had, through his interactions with the Dakotas, already become acquainted with the men and women who would impress him further by risking their lives to save white settlers.

The bishop had left the reservation in mid-July, first to return to his home in Faribault, where he had built a house on land he acquired in 1860 through generous donations from welcoming townspeople. After he had departed the reservation, the situation continued to deteriorate. The reservation appeared to lack a figure who could bridge the growing gap between the Dakotas, especially the younger men, and white officials. The latter tended to lack imagination and initiative when it came to recognizing the situation into which the Dakotas—so dependent on a payment that had not come—had been thrust. In early August, a hungry crowd broke into a government warehouse at the Upper Sioux Agency, touching off a tense standoff with soldiers billeted there. Under a compromise devised by a military officer, the Indian agent James Galbraith distributed some food and other supplies ahead of the expected payment. But at the Lower Sioux Agency an attempt by Little Crow—long known for his ability to work with whites—to broker a compromise with Galbraith failed. The chief, aware of the hunger on the reservation, demanded that traders at the Lower Sioux Agency extend the Indians credit until the annuity arrived. The traders gathered at the meeting refused, a response that inevitably harmed Little Crow's standing. One trader in particular—Andrew Myrick—made himself notorious by tossing off what would become an infamous insult to add to the injuries the Dakotas felt. With exceptional callousness, he declared in the Dakotas' presence that if the Indians were hungry, he would "let them eat grass." (By some accounts, Myrick actually said "dung" or a ruder synonym.) When the remark was translated for them, the Indians responded with loud and angry whoops. Myrick became a man marked for retribution, and his insult became one of the most-remembered statements of the entire war.

Galbraith might have realized that the annuity system was breaking down on the Dakota reservation. In addition to the disappointment caused by the delayed payment and the hunger experienced by some of the Indians, the Dakotas held another grievance the agent regularly encountered. They had come to believe that white officials had made, and then broken, a promise for their future welfare. During one of the treaties they had signed, the Dakotas became convinced that the agreements included annual provisions to each family of a blanket, gun, ammunition, and delicacies such as coffee, tea, and tobacco. Galbraith, the government agent, said individual Dakotas continually referred to these provisions in speeches and regarded their lack of fulfillment as "a perpetual source of complaint, discontent, and annoyance."[26] The Indian agent seemed unaware of how the discontent around him might explode into violence. As late as August 15—only three days before the Dakota War began—Galbraith passed a peaceful visit with Little Crow, and he thought the chief content. Little Crow had a small but newly built frame house. The agent later recorded the chief as saying "he had a store, a yoke of oxen, a wagon, and plenty of corn and potatoes, and was now living more comfortably than ever before."[27] The satisfaction that Galbraith perceived was very shallow.

Whipple took himself temporarily out of that picture when he journeyed north to visit the Ojibwes in early August. Had he reversed the order of his two pastoral visits—going to see the Ojibwes first, the Dakotas next—he might have found himself on the latter's reservation just when the killings at Acton threw the Mdewakantons into crisis. Instead, conducting the visits as he did, he missed seeing the collapse of an unhappy status quo for the Dakotas, one that had endured for a decade.

In contrast to his experience among the Dakotas, he described his time among the Ojibwes as exhilarating. He brought along Enmegahbowh to serve as his translator. Whipple also brought two canoes; in one, Enmegahbowh sat directly behind the bishop. They had seven companions. A priest, Rev. E. Steele Peake, who had served white settlers and Native Americans alike, rode in the second canoe. A sutler—a civilian employed by the army to provide goods—came along. So, too, did two Christian Indians and three other Native Americans, who followed traditional beliefs. The group carried fishing poles, and Enmegahbowh packed a shotgun, bringing down birds on the wing to supplement their dinners.

Whipple knew the route: it was the one he had taken during his first journey to the Ojibwes in 1859. He saw men and women with whom he had become acquainted through repeated visits. He listened to their concerns, the anxiety of their chiefs about white traders selling whiskey to their young men, and their fear that government agents wanted to do them out of their lands and timber. The bishop went primarily to preach, to affirm men and women who had already converted to Christianity and to try to reach those he wished would do so. But he also came as a friend, a public advocate for Native Americans.

He kept a diary, and its entries show him focused on the present and the pleasure of the tasks at hand, rather than the trouble he had experienced among the Dakotas. His words call to mind the power of close observation and sheer delight in the wilderness that would characterize the writings of the naturalist John Muir some years later. Whipple listened to the birds, paid heed to the flowers, even studied the flow of the water beneath his canoe. Two days into his trip, he reported that he and his companions had risen at four in the morning and taken their canoes out into a winding channel that passed from lake to lake; they paddled by acres of wild rice and admired clusters of white and yellow lilies afloat on the sunstruck waters. "God be praised for this glorious day!" the bishop declared. By their fourth day out, with the sun setting in a crystalline sky, Whipple wrote that the oncoming night contained a "stillness unbroken save by the hooting of an owl, the cry of a loon, or the bark of some wild beast." Their party rose again at four, their habit now, knelt to say prayers, then sat down on whatever was handy to eat breakfast. Whipple, looking out across his canoe's bow, saw "thousands of acres" of wild rice. They took a twisting channel, cutting through marsh grasses that seemed to want to enclose them. Fields of lilies again floated before them. The next morning, back on the water shortly after dawn, they entered a lake they thought beautiful. They canoed past a point of land and found themselves in a place where the natural acoustics produced what Whipple called "a wonderful echo."[28] And, he wrote, "[w]e saw quantities of the wild plum, cherries, currants, gooseberries, whortle and blueberries; also black and red cherries, and the finest hazelnuts I ever saw."

After five days on the water, the party reached a point at which they beached their canoes for the overland trek to reach Red Lake, about a hundred miles from where they had originally started. This meant a fifteen-mile hike over uneven, often marshy terrain. The bishop turned an ankle but limped gamely on. Along the way, they encountered a French Canadian, a former fur trader named Shubway who had truly taken to the woods, living there nearly forty years. That Sunday he let the bishop use his house to celebrate Communion. The bishop held a service for the Ojibwes, who crowded into the room or gathered at the door and windows. He felt moved by his congregation's solemnity. It overwhelmed his reaction to what he called their "grotesque" ornamentation. "Every variety of ornament was worn; several had the entire rim of the ear slit off. . . . They were all in blankets, paint, and feathers." He kept his sermon simple: "[T]he love of Jesus Christ with its practical application, that the object of the gospel was to show men how to live in this world so that they would be fit to live in the Great Spirit's Home hereafter."[29] He later wrote that he had concluded that Ojibwe religious beliefs emphasized the here and now, making it difficult to put across the Christian concept of an afterlife in paradise.[30]

Later, with the Ojibwe chief, Whipple took out his letter to Lincoln and read it aloud. As always when he criticized the government's Office of Indian Affairs, Whipple scrupulously avoided naming individuals, even those he perceived as particularly corrupt and venal. But despite the omission, he possessed sufficient material to present his case. He made it clear he believed from what he had seen that Native Americans—and not just in Minnesota—had been treated with appalling dishonesty, essentially robbed, plied with liquor, and left to fend for themselves. He laid the blame on a highly politicized Indian Affairs office that in all practicality served the interests of its officials rather than the Indians. It was the spoils system, run rampant, thieves appointed to supervise thieves. Whipple offered blunt, critical analysis that he would use often to make his point: "The Indian agents who are placed in trust of the honor and faith of the government are generally selected without any reference to their fitness for the place. The congressional delegation desire to reward John Doe for party work, and John Doe desires the place because there is a tradition on the border that an Indian agent with Fifteen hundred dollars a year can retire on an ample fortune in four years."[31] In Whipple's view, work that should have meant service to Native American tribes amounted to avaricious scheming by men who wanted nothing more than to get rich very quickly.

"Every employee," he wrote, with reference to the Office of Indian Affairs, "ought to be a man of purity, temperance, industry, and unquestioned integrity. Those selected to teach in any department must be men of peculiar fitness, patient, quick perceptions, enlarged ideas, and men who love their work." Whipple wrote that the Indians must be accorded protection under American laws; the government ought to build them houses and provide them with agricultural tools. It ought also to build schools for them. Whipple proposed that Lincoln appoint a commission—of prominent men, but not politicians— who would investigate the Indian Affairs office and recommend specific reforms.

The Ojibwe chief reacted with pleasure to the letter, Whipple would later recall. He escorted the bishop on a tour of the tribe's agricultural work, where Whipple saw the evidence of tilling and planting that he regarded as fundamental to creating a new economy for Native Americans. The sight impressed him, confirming his belief that a form of Indian self-sufficiency, based on agriculture, lay close at hand. "We rode four miles on the banks of the lake, and I never saw a more beautiful sight than these gardens, extending for miles. There is hardly a lodge which has not corn of last year. In one lodge we counted twenty-nine sacks of old corn. Everywhere there were signs of plenty." The party ate new potatoes and green corn from the Indian gardens. Yet Whipple felt troubled. His hosts were under pressure to sell their land. He feared that if that happened, it would plunge the Ojibwes into a dependency he saw among the Dakotas.[32]

Without specifically naming the Dakotas by way of comparison, he wrote, "The condition of these people is so unlike that of the Indians in treaty relations with the Government, that one cannot fail to see at a glance the iniquity of which lies at the door of the Government." Before he left Red Lake, he added: "As I looked into the anxious face of the chief, I could not help a great throb of pity for the helpless man who felt the pressure of a stronger power, knowing that he must sell and yet fearing that the sale of his land to a great Christian nation would be his people's doom." It moved Whipple to prayer: "God in mercy pity a people thus wronged, and help them!"[33]

Two

The First Attack

REV. SAMUEL HINMAN MAY HAVE BEEN THE FIRST white person to see Chief Little Crow the morning of August 18 and also live to tell about it. Fewer than five miles lay between the chief's village and the Lower Sioux Agency, where Hinman served Bishop Whipple, supervising the Episcopal mission of Saint John. At sunrise that morning hundreds of Dakota men streamed across that distance to lay siege to the agency, an indefensible collection of government buildings.

Hinman, appointed missionary priest by the bishop in 1860, had a gentle appearance, but his soft, dark eyes, set in an oval face, his jaw fringed by a carefully trimmed beard, belied a nature of fierce determination. In the previous two years, he had grown deeply attached to the Dakotas and his work among them. An orphan who grew up in Connecticut, Hinman came west as a young man to Minnesota, where he studied for the Episcopal Church priesthood. Whipple had ordained him and sent him to the Dakota reservation. Seven weeks before the attack, Hinman stood with Whipple when the bishop laid the cornerstone for what both men expected would be a permanent church structure, evidence of the diocese of Minnesota's commitment to the tribe.[1]

The day of the attack, the young priest had risen early. He planned to leave shortly for Faribault on church business; he had sent his wife and infant child ahead. He had eaten his breakfast and taken a seat on the steps of the two-year-old mission house to pass a little time with a carpenter, arrived to begin the day's work on the church building. Already the walls stood in place; the roof would come next. As the men chatted, an explosion of rifle fire split the morning air. Minutes later, Hinman spotted Little Crow at a run, dashing toward the agency's barn. Hinman had long known the chief. Moreover, he had seen him among his own congregation the morning before. Little Crow—known and respected as a practitioner of traditional Dakota beliefs and medicine—had politely shaken hands all around after the service. Now, stripped for battle, the chief seemed a man transformed. Hinman called out to him, asking what was happening. Little Crow looked abruptly away. In so doing, he sent Hinman a signal—a plain, if nonverbal, warning—that effectively saved the priest's life. Within seconds, Hinman was on his feet, running for safety amidst the engulfing violence.[2]

Of the principal figures in the Dakota War, Little Crow stands out as singularly pitiable. No other prominent participant in the Dakota War was targeted for so much individual blame by white Minnesotans or perceived to change so radically in temperament and action as Little Crow. He had gone to bed the previous night known as a man inclined to negotiate with whites, even if he felt dissatisfied with the results. Hours later he rose to embark on a warrior's trajectory that would earn him a hated reputation in Minnesota. Politicians, newspaper editors, and settlers alike would count him as the primary aggressor in a war that, initially at least, targeted civilians.

The chief's transformation began with an argument among Dakota men—an echo of what had happened in Acton, but with a larger cast and higher stakes. Brown Wing and his companions, the four young men who had killed the settlers in Acton, had returned to Rice Creek Village on Sunday evening, where word of their violence had excited men to take the news to Shakopee, whose village lay nearby. Amidst the ensuing discussions, talk increasingly turned toward fighting, striking first at the whites who were deemed certain to demand harsh punishment for the Acton killings. Before the idea of a swift, surprise blow could be carried further, Shakopee wanted someone prominent to agree to join the cause, a figure capable of rallying a greater number of Dakotas. He and the others sought out Chief Little Crow and argued for war.

Little Crow had received plaudits from government officials and others who passed through his village, Kaposia. Visitors tended to describe the chief as a dignified and generous host with a keen, inquiring intellect. On a frontier of both Native Americans and whites given to destructive alcohol consumption, Little Crow advocated sobriety. (The stance placed him in the temperance camp with Whipple and Stephen Riggs, a Presbyterian missionary who had worked among the Dakotas for a quarter century before the war.) In middle age, the chief impressed the whites he met as physically robust, athletic beyond his years, and possessing a strong, even admirable character. Dr. Asa Daniels, a physician Whipple admired for his commitment to the Dakotas, recalled meeting Little Crow in June 1854. He estimated the chief then to be about forty, standing five feet ten inches tall and weighing about a hundred and sixty pounds. Daniels thought Little Crow "restless and active, intelligent, of strong personality, of great physical vigor."[3] The doctor had been appointed by the Office of Indian Affairs during the Democratic presidency of Franklin Pierce to serve the two Dakota bands living near the Lower Sioux Agency. Early on, Daniels encountered Little Crow as a patient. The chief, leading a group of the elderly, women, and children, had come under attack by a small party of Ojibwes armed with buckshot. Afterward, Little Crow went to see Daniels to have his wounds treated.[4]

Daniels found the chief to be affable and self-possessed, but he also thought him arrogant (a reaction that may very well have originated in his encountering such a self-confident non-white). Little Crow, he thought, was "vainly confident of his own superiority and that of his people." The chief wore a record of his military prowess: "His head was decorated with three eagle feathers, notched and dyed, indicating his early exploits on the war-path." Daniels also noticed that Little Crow carried deep scars from old wounds: "Both wrists were badly deformed from fracture of the bones by gunshot wounds." But the doctor thought Little Crow "had good use of his hands."[5] Daniels lived on the reservation for six years. During that time, he came to see that Little Crow had a great fondness for children. The chief's eldest son, Wowinape, was his "great pride," presented by Little Crow as his successor. When Daniels's wife gave birth to their daughter, the chief paid a visit, bringing meat and wild rice. He gave the infant a pet name and snuggled her in his arms.

In his years as a reservation physician, Daniels also learned about Little Crow's background and how his wrists had been injured. The chief could boast a distinguished lineage among the Mdewakantons, the "People of Spirit Lake," who formed the easternmost band of the Dakotas. Little Crow grew up in Kaposia, a seasonal village, originally located on the east bank of the Mississippi River near present-day Saint Paul. His family gave him the name Taoyateduta, translated as His Red Nation. His grandfather, Chetanwakhuwamani, and his father, Wakin-yantanka, had each in his turn served as village chief and had gotten on well with whites, whom they principally knew as explorers, military men, and fur traders, not as crowds of permanent settlers, who came later. Both men had also been called Little Crow by the whites who passed through the region and learned that the family leaders carried a crow's skin and wore it as a sacred adornment. Daniels described the bird as the family's totem, "the skin of which was carefully prepared to represent the bird in repose, and was worn [in] back of and below the right shoulder."[6]

Little Crow's grandfather and father signed treaties ceding land to the federal government, substantial tracts of the future state of Minnesota. Chetanwakhuwamani agreed to sell the early-nineteenth-century explorer Zebulon Pike a militarily strategic tract at the confluence of the Mississippi and Minnesota rivers. In 1819, the government built a military installation there and named it Fort Snelling. Little Crow's father, Wakinyantanka, proved even more generous, signing a treaty in 1837 that parted with nearly five million acres of largely Mdewakanton territory on the Mississippi's eastern bank. Relatively few of the band lived there, but the transaction placed Kaposia in a border area where the village would be exposed to white culture once the ceded lands were sold and settled.[7] Wakinyantanka moved the village across the Mississippi to the river's western bank, yet it still sat on a highly porous boundary, across which all manner of trade—especially liquor—moved.

It was in the relocated village that Wakinyantanka died prematurely and violently, an incident that brought his son Little Crow directly into the historical narrative. Following a moving wagon uphill one day, Wakinyantanka noticed that his rifle, piled among other items in the wagon, had begun to slide out. He impulsively reached for it, hit the trigger, and suffered a terrible wound. He lay dying in his lodge for three days. Just before death he anointed one of his many sons, a half-brother of Little Crow, as his successor. But Little Crow—then living further west among other Dakota bands on the Minnesota River—returned to his home village upon hearing the news. The story brims with visual drama. At Kaposia, villagers rushed to the riverbank to see Little Crow arrive by canoe. Some shouted for him to turn back. Others warned him that he risked death from his half-brothers if he stepped ashore. Demonstrating physical courage, Little Crow replied, "Shoot then, where we all can see.

I am not afraid and they all know it." He folded his hands across his chest, crossing his wrists, one atop the other. An unarmed man faced would-be assassins. A supporter of one of his half-brothers fired, striking Little Crow and knocking him backward into the arms of a friend.

Little Crow's friends rushed him upriver to Fort Snelling, where an army doctor examined his wounds and recommended both hands be amputated. But Little Crow rejected the advice and asked to be brought back to Kaposia, where he was entrusted to a village shaman and gradually recovered. The bullet would leave him permanently disfigured (the scars Daniels observed), but Little Crow prevailed. The village rallied to him as the new chief. (The half-brothers shortly turned up dead.)[8]

Little Crow's decision not to undergo amputation did not surprise the Presbyterian missionary Thomas Williamson, a longtime resident in the region. In an essay he later contributed to an ethnographic study of the Dakotas, he reported that the tribe deeply resisted the idea of such an operation. "I have heard individuals, to whom it was proposed, declare that they would rather die than have an arm or foot cut off."[9]

No one suggested the injury negatively affected Little Crow's status in his village. A decade later, James Lynd described Little Crow—then living on the Dakota reservation—as "dignified and commanding." Lynd, a former Minnesota state legislator, lived at the Lower Sioux Agency at the time the war erupted, working as a trader in Andrew Myrick's store. He spoke Dakota and had completed a long manuscript, which he hoped to sell, about the tribe's life and religion. Lynd thought that at times Little Crow seemed "restless and anxious." He also noted the chief's "sharp features, . . . piercing hazel eye[s]," and bold forehead.[10]

By contrast, Bishop Whipple said little about the chief, at least in his writing. But the bishop's relative silence had a practical origin. Whipple viewed the Dakota War through a broader lens, the same lens he had applied to the Indians' situation since he had arrived in Minnesota. It set him apart from many of his fellow whites before the war and afterward. Whipple attributed the war's cause to human greed; the federal government's venality in running a dangerously corrupt Indian affairs system had triggered the violence. Indian policy lured incompetent, self-seeking men and placed them where they could do singular harm to Indians and, by extension, all who lived near them. This thinking allowed Whipple to maintain a perspective different from that of his neighbors, many of whom would seek a racist explanation for the war. In the popular version, Indians were untrustworthy savages, and many whites would link Little Crow personally with those attributes.

After midnight on August 18, the group of young Dakota men from Rice Creek and Shakopee's villages shouldered their way into the wood-framed house that white officials at the agency had built for Little Crow.[11] They roused the chief and broke the news about the murders in Acton. Several among the visitors laid out a simple, violent plan. The Dakotas, they urged, should wage all-out war against Minnesota's white settlers—and they wanted Little Crow with them. Could there be a better time to strike? The Civil War had drained able-bodied men from the frontier into the ranks of distant federal armies. Those armies, fighting hundreds of miles away, seemed only to lose. The illustrated newspapers showed that much.

Little Crow heard the young men out with grave misgiving and pleas for peace. He blackened his face and covered his head with a cloth as a sign of mourning.[12] From his own experience of whites outside Minnesota, he knew these uninvited Dakota men dangerously underestimated the people they wanted to fight. Twice he had traveled to Washington and shaken hands with a president, once with Franklin Pierce and once with James Buchanan. He had slept in a New York hotel and taken the railroad to Niagara Falls. He had become familiar with the vastness of the white population and the power of its technology. Once, he appealed to Asa Daniels for support when Dakota friends openly doubted Little Crow's story of how fast a train could go. In councils where Dakota men gathered, Little Crow held aloft a large print of Boston, which he had borrowed from the doctor. A panoramic view of the city as seen from Bunker Hill, it portrayed thousands of houses and commercial buildings scattered around the harbor. Whites, Little Crow stated, were thickly settled, their numbers immense by Dakota standards, fully capable of supplying fighting men to battle even if their enemies slaughtered the first wave of their advance.[13]

Little Crow's knowledge carried no weight with his visitors on August 18. He sat before men who wanted blood and wanted him with them when they spilled it. The argument raged on, tempers rising, until nearly sunrise. Finally, one young man, impudent with excitement, dared to call Little Crow a coward. The insult cut the chief deeply; he struck his accuser, knocking the man's feathered headdress to the floor. He then let loose the oratory that had for years served him as a revered spokesman among the Santee. He called the younger men fools and accused them of being drunk. Listen, he said, "the white men are like locusts when they fly so thick that the whole sky is a snowstorm." The Dakotas might kill many, but that would not restore the past. "Kill one—two—ten, and ten times ten will come to kill you. Count your fingers all day long and white men with guns will come faster than you can count."[14] As Little Crow spoke, his son, Wowinape, stood at his side, memorizing the speech. He would recall his father, in a spirit of lamentation, pronouncing the young men blind and deaf to his sagacity. "You cannot see the face of your chief; your eyes are full of smoke. You cannot hear his voice; your ears are full of roaring waters." Little Crow, who until very recently had held the office of speaker for the tribe, summoned a natural eloquence to talk them out of further violence. He predicted they would surely die "like the rabbits when the hungry wolves hunt them" in winter. But Little Crow would join them, he said. And in doing so, he added, he expected to die too.

The chief's warning of ultimate defeat would ring true, but his prophecy of the Dakotas' destruction in battle initially proved off the mark. The men who went to war that morning had surprise on their side. Even so, Little Crow grasped the overall result and its consequences: death and the end of the life of the Mdewakantons as they had known it.

Writing after the war, Samuel Pond, a veteran Minnesota missionary, said that if Little Crow had lived a generation earlier, "he probably would have been an active and successful hunter, and would have passed through life without doing much harm."[15] Or at least the harm for which he might be remembered would have been minor. Gary Clayton Anderson, author of the most thorough and dispassionate biography of Little Crow, said that the chief might have thought that by joining the men so hungry for a war, he would be able to exert some control over how it proceeded.[16] A close reading of the war's events suggests Little Crow maintained an ambiguous attitude toward individual whites, even to the extent of protecting some prisoners.[17] That attitude was evident in the incident that morning with Hinman, in which he aborted their eye contact.

Moments after Hinman saw Little Crow, he heard a gunshot close by. The men who came rampaging into the agency's grounds had opened fire. In the barn, a Dakota soldier brought down a government employee, A. H. Wagner, who had run in to prevent the Indians from taking the horses. Wagner served as superintendent of farms and worked closely with the so-called farmer Indians, families who had taken up agriculture. On them, Whipple and others had pinned hopes for a change in the Dakota economy. Mortally wounded, Wagner sprawled near the body of John Lamb, a teamster, killed while trying to flee.

But the first shot Hinman had heard—the one that preceded Little Crow's appearance—cut down Myrick's employee, James Lynd. The Dakotas had fascinated him; he had devoted years to their study. He kept his manuscript in the store, where an undamaged portion—about Dakota religion—would be discovered weeks later. As the first to fall, Lynd symbolized how complicated the Dakota War would be: never a simple case of one easily defined side against another. A Kentucky native and former newspaper editor, Lynd had taken a keen interest in Dakota society. He had spoken their language, said the missionary Thomas Williamson, "with ease and fluency and so associate[d] with them as to acquire their confidence, and thus learn from themselves their traditions and mythology." Lynd had also had a keen sense of the tribe's decentralized political life. "Neither the nation, nor the different tribes of the Dakotas are governed by any one chief or ruler," he wrote. "Each tribe is divided into numerous bands; and each one of these bands has its own particular chief. . . . It often happens, however, that a chief of one band, by his talents in speaking, bravery, or other superior faculty, becomes more widely known and more respected than the others; and in such case, he is looked up to by the remaining chiefs—though it cannot be said that he is chief of the tribe."[18] In essence, Lynd described Little Crow, whose authority was never as permanent or as all encompassing as the whites who later blamed him for the war would have it.

Hinman, fleeing after his encounter with Little Crow, took a path back through the mission house. He encountered Emily West, a Christian teacher resident among the Dakotas, and told her to run for it. West had heard the first gunshots as she washed up the dishes after breakfast. Amidst the noise and confusion, the two were soon separated.

Hinman got to safety across the Minnesota River and would later tell Whipple that, just before he had taken to his heels, he had encountered a Dakota who seemed to want to stop the attack right there. That man was named Sunkaska—in English, White Dog—and his actions that day would always be framed by an ambiguity that eventually cost him his life. In those first few minutes, White Dog told Hinman that men with "bad hearts" were fanning out across the agency to kill; he, White Dog, would find Chief Wabasha, a man known for his peaceful inclinations, and ask him to intercede to stop the killing.[19]

Emily West also ran toward the river, along the way meeting a woman and two children, whose ages she remembered as nine and eleven. The four of them passed several Indians, who ignored them. One Dakota shot and killed a white man who was struggling to save his horse. The women and children slid down the bluffs and made it to the small ferry stationed just below the agency. The boatman (who soon died at his post) cast off and landed them on the river's north side.

Ironically, a war party saved Emily West. She owed her life—along with that of the three others—to a group of Dakotas who came upon her as the agency was overrun. She later told the story: "[T]o avoid the river, along which the road to Fort Ridgely ran, we struck off, two or three miles, in the prairie." They spotted a log house and, thinking it a safe haven, began to rush toward it. Four Dakota men appeared and cut them off. For West and her companions, that might have been the end. But her role at the agency worked to protect her. "When they came to us, they recognized me, called me a missionary, and said I was good. I offered them my hand; they shook hands with me, told me they were going to that house, that we must not go there, but to the Fort, pointed the way and left us. We afterward heard of their killing the inmates of that house."[20] West, the other woman, and the two children reached Fort Ridgley about ten hours later, "under the protection and guidance of our Heavenly Father," she said. They found Hinman already there. He had taken a different route and reached the fort earlier in the day.

At least twenty people at the agency—nearly a third of its population—did not fare as well. They died in the violence that swept around them. After Lynd's death, Dakota soldiers shot another of Myrick's clerks, George Divoll. Andrew Myrick was in the building when the attack began. He had the presence of mind to jump from a second-floor window and run pell-mell toward a ravine that descended to the river. He saw the trees and brush in which he could hide, but he never made it. Days later, when white soldiers recovered his body, they found the Dakotas had jammed fistfuls of grass into the trader's gaping mouth—an unmistakable reply to Myrick's brutish insult of the hunger-racked Indians two weeks earlier. Other traders and clerks died at their counters or as they tried to flee. Crossing the river did not guarantee safety. On the Minnesota's north side, a group of armed Dakotas encountered the agency's doctor, with his wife and children, and dispatched them all. Others killed a man known to the Dakotas for decades, Philander Prescott, who had lived and traded among them and earned his keep as a government translator. He had married a Dakota woman.

Even when caught in the direst circumstances, some whites survived—like Emily West—depending on whom they knew. George Spencer, a clerk wounded in the assault on a trader's building, managed to pull himself up the stairs and onto a bed while Dakota soldiers looted the stores on the ground floor. Spencer later reckoned he spent an hour waiting to be discovered and murdered where he lay, but then, he said, "I heard the voice of an Indian inquiring for me." He recognized the voice and felt a confidence spread over him that he would be all right after all. A noted soldier named Wakinyantawa ascended to Spencer's bedside, asked how badly he was hurt, and then physically helped him descend the stairs. Several Dakotas froze in place then loudly demanded that Spencer be killed on the spot, but Wakinyantawa stopped them. As he escorted Spencer to the door, he told his fellow Dakota, "If you had killed him before I saw him, it would have been all right; but we have been friends and comrades for ten years, and now that I have seen him, I will protect him or die with him."[21] Spencer survived the war in a Dakota camp and was later released to the care of federal soldiers.

Smaller attacks bloodied the surrounding countryside. Settler families, singly or in groups, fell victim to acts of violence, occasionally from Native Americans they knew. Their narratives make for terrifying reading—astonishing, too, given the remarkable capability of wounded and traumatized people to survive. Some walked days to find rescue. David Carrothers, who lived on Beaver Creek in Renville County, heard of the attacks and joined twenty-six men, women, and children who banded together to seek safety.[22] Abandoning their farms on the flatland north of the Minnesota River, nearly opposite the agency, they fled across the prairie. One boy among them carried a weapon belonging to Little Crow, a long gun the chief had given as security three days earlier when he purchased a cow from a farmer named Jonathan Earle, a Vermont native who had arrived on the land only two months earlier. "It was a splendid gun and was reluctantly left as a pawn," his son, Ezmon, then seventeen, would recall. The group traveled little more than a mile before a group of about twenty Dakotas, riding horses, intercepted them. The Indians told them they had come out to kill white settlers. Carrothers and his companions quickly tried to barter, offering their horses in return for their lives, but the group was in a poor position to negotiate, and the Indians began shooting. The Dakotas appeared intent on capturing the women and children; the men fled on foot. Young Ezmon Earle saw Carrothers's five-year-old son killed.

No one could really have known what might happen when parties of Dakotas encountered whites. August Gluth, a twelve-year-old from a German immigrant family, lost his older brother that day, but the boy himself survived—in part, thanks to Little

Crow. Gluth, spending the summer tending cattle near Beaver Falls, became a captive of a group of Indians who took him and the animals to Little Crow's village. Once there, Gluth was ordered to handle ox teams that parties of Indians had stolen from nearby farms. Young Gluth later testified that Little Crow intervened to save his life when another Dakota caught the boy trying to escape from the village. It was Gluth's second attempt, and the man who stopped him appeared ready to kill him with a tomahawk, until Little Crow told him not to do so.[23] His story contributes to the ambiguity that seems to cling to Little Crow in the war. What did he believe would be achieved, as the fighting went on?

On the war's first day, Little Crow's soldiers took Susan Brown and several of her children captive. A member of the Sisseton band of the Dakotas and wife of the former Indian agent, Joseph Brown, she eventually ended up an unwilling guest in Little Crow's house. As her grandson George Allanson recalled later, Little Crow came and spoke privately with her. He told her he had tried initially to prevent a war. However, when he could not, "he entered into the project and was bending all his energies to its success." Allanson also recalled Little Crow telling Brown that the war "was bound to come anyway, as the Indians had no redress for the injuries done to them . . ."[24]

The Dakotas struck hard in those first few days, fairly destroying the Lower Sioux Agency, killing more than fifty people in the little town of New Milford and twice besieging New Ulm, on the river's south bank, and the federal installation Fort Ridgely on the north. In New Ulm, a largely German outpost developed in the late 1850s, local leadership and a determined citizenry barely kept the attackers at bay. But the cost, at the end of two battles, was the destruction of much of the town. Its defenders deliberately burned its buildings to deny the Indians shelter during the attacks. Soldiers and civilians at Fort Ridgely, poorly designed to withstand an assault and by then swollen with refugees, managed to keep the Dakotas from seizing the main buildings.

Soldiers from Ridgely attempted to relieve the Lower Sioux Agency that first day of the war. A man named Dickinson, who fled the agency early, reached the fort and told its senior officer, Captain John Marsh, about the attack. Marsh, a veteran of the Union army in its disastrous defeat at the first Battle of Bull Run the previous year, gathered nearly fifty soldiers. Out on the road, they met Hinman, coming the other way. The missionary, believing the soldiers would be outnumbered, tried to talk Marsh out of it, but the captain disregarded the warning and took his command up the river directly to a site across from the agency. By then, the ferryman had been killed, but the little craft remained at the riverbank. On the opposite bank, Marsh spotted White Dog, the Indian who had told Hinman he wanted to stop the attack. What happened then remains open to dispute. Marsh brought up an interpreter to try to learn what he would face across the river. Soldiers would later remember White Dog urging them to cross; the Indian denied that, saying he tried to warn them they were in grave danger. The conversation did not last long, interrupted by almost point-blank gunshots as Marsh and his command came under an ambush attack from Dakotas who had staked out positions in the riverside brush. The captain lost twenty-three men and died in the river, drowning as he attempted to swim to safety.[25]

Survivors trickled back to Ridgely, bringing news of the disaster. Word of the engagement also traveled upriver, where it appalled the Dakotas who opposed the war. One man, a Christian named Taopi, who would emerge as a leading figure among a group that became known as the peace party, had planned that morning to visit Hinman at the agency. Instead, he wound up watching the attack from the roof of his house. As the hours passed, Dakota men put the agency's buildings to the torch, sending up a dark plume visible for miles across the prairie.

Taopi learned through a friend "that nearly a whole company of soldiers from the fort had been killed at the ferry." He had had a plan to take white settlers to safety, but he decided it would have to wait as now the escape route had been cut off.[26]

In launching their attack that morning, the Dakota soldiers had counted on surprise and the advantage of many young white men being away fighting in the Civil War, resulting in the Minnesota River Valley possessing only light defenses. But Little Crow and his allies also faced a problem that only grew as their war went on. Never did the four bands of the Santee Dakotas unite in overt hostility to the whites—the war began and ended primarily as a Mdewakanton project. Furthermore, even some among the Mdewakanton band sympathized with the whites, especially those they had grown to know as neighbors, and more than a few risked their lives to protect them. As a result, some whites survived amidst very dangerous circumstances and later reported they owed their lives to individual Dakotas. Among those saviors, some Mdewakantons had held long friendships with the men, women, and children they rescued. Others acted on the spot.

Up and down the river, from August 18 until the fighting ended five weeks later, whites encountered Dakotas who vehemently disapproved of the war, a few of them blunt enough to say that to Little Crow himself. But on the war's first day, the attackers held the upper hand, quickly overrunning the Lower Sioux Agency. Smaller groups of Dakota soldiers attacked elsewhere among the Minnesota River settlements, spreading out the conflict like a bloodstain across the bluffs and prairies on either side of the river. Settlers died, taken by surprise; others watched as death approached them, often at a runner's pace, gun or hatchet in hand.

Three

Lincoln and the Indians

HENRY WHIPPLE RECEIVED NEWS OF THE DAKOTA WAR a day after the attack on the Lower Sioux Agency, home to his priest Samuel Hinman and the Episcopal Church mission. Within little more than four weeks, the bishop met with President Lincoln and elaborated his understanding of how the war came to be, laying out an argument for a thorough overhaul of the federal Indian office. By then, Lincoln had heard angry, even desperate, accounts of the Dakotas' warfare from Minnesota's governor, Alexander Ramsey; General John Pope, whom the president had dispatched to lead military operations against the Dakotas; and Lincoln's personal secretary, John Nicolay, who had been traveling in the state when the war occurred. Without seeing any of their correspondence to Lincoln, Whipple readily guessed their words, which reflected increasingly shrill accounts of the war in the state's newspapers. For Whipple to lobby Lincoln on Indian affairs at this moment could mean placing his project at risk. The president might send him on his way. But Whipple did not think that would happen. He had another idea of the man in whom he would place his trust for a change of governmental practice toward Native Americans.

The bishop had an intuition about Abraham Lincoln, based

on what he had read and heard so far about the president. As bishop, Whipple spent far more time writing to Lincoln than about him. But much later, he would describe his confidence in getting a successful hearing at the White House. That confidence rested on two bases. First, Whipple understood Lincoln as essentially empathetic, and thus willing to listen to him on behalf of a people who had suffered historic abuse. Second, he knew the president had experience with white–Indian warfare. Lincoln had written about it—albeit very briefly, and without any sense of triumphalism or denigration of the Indians involved. What's more, the absence of such rhetoric was all the more notable, given that Lincoln had publicly said that his own family had suffered great loss in an Indian raid. His paternal grandfather, after whom he was named, had died unarmed, taken by surprise by an Indian rifleman hidden near where he was planting crops.

Whipple did not begin as an admirer of Lincoln, even though Illinois senator Stephen Douglas, Lincoln's principal opponent in the 1860 election, had told the bishop not to underestimate the man. Their conversation took place in the politically heightened atmosphere of Chicago in May 1860, as the Republican Party prepared to convene there to nominate a presidential candidate. Only months earlier Whipple had bid Chicago good-bye and moved to Minnesota to take up his new duties, but now he was back in Chicago on a visit. A parishioner at his former church, William McAlpine, took him to meet Douglas. McAlpine was a railroad executive and, like Whipple, a Democrat. During their meeting with Douglas, talk inevitably turned to politics. The senator offered his opinion that the Republicans would be "wise" to nominate Lincoln as their presidential candidate. That surprised McAlpine, as it likely did Whipple too. The bishop had lived in the city two years earlier during the great Lincoln–Douglas contest over a seat in the U.S. Senate. Did Douglas actually think Lincoln "fit to be president"? McAlpine asked.

Douglas responded by praising Lincoln's political skills. "You know I have been a public speaker ever since I came to Illinois," Douglas said, "and I have never met so able an opponent as Abraham Lincoln."[1]

Regardless of Douglas's appraisal, it took Whipple only a few months to begin to have his doubts about Lincoln's personal depth and abilities. After the election, the bishop let friends know he did not think Lincoln a sufficiently serious man to deal with the crisis of secession ripping the United States asunder. By February 1861, the month before Lincoln took office, no fewer than seven Southern states had declared themselves seceded from the Union. On February 4, they formed their own federation, adopting a constitution. Two weeks later, they chose a president, Jefferson Davis, a former U.S. senator from Mississippi. Whipple told a friend soon afterward, "I see little but thick darkness ahead."[2] That comment did not necessarily reflect his view of Lincoln, but it came close to what he wrote about the incoming president in other letters that month. Whipple had never met Lincoln. Part of the problem, then, lay in the bishop's perception of the public man, as portrayed in the newspapers.

As the secession crisis accelerated, Lincoln prepared for his journey from his home in Springfield, Illinois, to Washington, DC. The journey would begin February 11, the day prior to his fifty-second birthday. As the date neared, he received an ever-growing list of invitations from Northern state legislatures, asking him to stop and speak to them along the way. Charting an itinerary to satisfy these requests resulted in a rambling—and personally fatiguing—cross-country route. As he made his way to Washington, he addressed large public audiences and much smaller, informal crowds that gathered to hear him. Lincoln used no single text and sometimes, as with the small gatherings, he spoke impromptu. His various statements made different impressions on the many who read them or read of them.

His style ranged from authoritative to homespun and warm. Many Unionists eventually became used to Lincoln's manner of speaking and recognized in him the deeply serious person he was, even when he told humorous stories to relieve stressful situations. (Whipple would have the same experience, in person.) But in early 1861, Lincoln's speeches and trackside greetings did not always translate into a completely coherent approach to the national crisis when they appeared in newsprint.

Lincoln's special train took him across central Indiana and Ohio to Pittsburgh, Pennsylvania, and back into Ohio, to Cleveland. He then traveled across upstate New York to Albany, turning south to New York City. From there, it was on to Trenton, New Jersey, and Philadelphia and Harrisburg, Pennsylvania. By the time he arrived in Washington, twelve days later, Lincoln had made ninety-three stops, an exhausting schedule. Crowds had grown very large along the way, interspersed with people so aggressively determined to see the new chief executive up close that Lincoln's staff and advisers feared for his safety. No one knew whether these seemingly rapturous audiences might contain an assassin.[3]

Whipple, reading of this journey from a distance of hundreds of miles, had no way to form an independent opinion. On February 23, the bishop wrote to his friend Napoleon Dana, the military officer turned banker whose endorsement helped persuade Minnesota Episcopalians to elect Whipple their bishop two years earlier. He lamented "our beloved country to human eyes rent in twain and on the eve of Civil Strife." Worse, he faulted Lincoln for not appearing to rise to the dreadful occasion. "The newly elected President seemingly lost to all sense of his responsibilities & going on a tour of pleasure, cracking jokes & indulging in pleasantries when a thoughtful man would be bowed to the earth in sorrow & calmly gathering every energy for a mighty effort to save the land from Civil War."[4]

Whipple could not know that Lincoln was, in his own way, "gathering every energy" to save the Union and to attempt first to do so peacefully. When Whipple read reports (and perhaps the reprinted text itself) of Lincoln's first inaugural address, he ought to have felt reassured. On March 4, Lincoln took the oath of office, and that same day, Whipple told a relative he hoped "a strong conservative element" would prevail in the new administration. He meant he hoped for Northern leaders who would not judge the life or death of slavery as the decisive issue in the unfolding conflict but would simply place saving the Union above all. In the North, that sentiment was common among all but abolitionists, who sought immediate emancipation of slaves. "It is doubtless the only hope for our beloved country," Whipple wrote.[5] Saving the Union without violence was the offer Lincoln made to the South in his inaugural speech.

But Whipple did not belong to the part of the Northern population that would accept peace at almost any price. The bishop's view of the crisis was formed as much by his theology as his political ideas. He had a biblically based horror of political rebellion. To break the covenant to maintain a democratic nation, as Southern secessionists were doing, was to provoke God's wrath. Had not Paul made this message clear, in the opening three verses of his Letter to the Romans, specifically in chapter 13? "Let every soul be subject unto the higher powers. For there is no power but of God: the powers that be are ordained of God. Whosoever therefore resisteth the power, resisteth the ordinance of God: and they that resist shall receive to themselves damnation. For rulers are not a terror to good works, but to the evil. Wilt thou then not be afraid of the power? Do that which is good, and thou shalt have praise of the same" (Rom. 13:1–3).

Whipple's reading of the Bible apparently did not persuade him to claim God's favor for the North, as many Northern clergy would do. He instead soon urged Northern soldiers to do their military duty to their nation in confronting the rebels. But he held to a distinction about humanity's relationship to God that eluded fellow pulpiteers who seemed in their preaching to focus on the utter righteousness of their region's cause. Whipple believed in the sovereignty of a God far beyond human reckoning. Men and women must be obedient to God, who remained ultimately in charge and not controlled by human prayers or wishes. Whipple stood theologically closer to Lincoln, at least as the president's religious thinking began to deepen from 1862 onward. Furthermore, the bishop maintained an acute consciousness of what he regarded as the nation's sins. God, he warned, despised mistreatment of the Indians in much the same way God considered African American slavery a grievous wrong.[6]

When the Civil War began, Whipple spoke out to the public about its moral duty (as he also would in the wake of the Dakota War). On April 17, four days after Union defenders surrendered Fort Sumter to a besieging Confederate force, Whipple wrote a pastoral letter to be read from the pulpits of every Episcopal Church in Minnesota. "Everything which the Christian and Patriot holds dear is in jeopardy. Our country's flag is dishonored. Our Government is defied. . . . The duty of the Christian is plain. We must be loyal to our Government. Our only hope in this day of peril, under the protection of Almighty God, is to stand firm as loyal and law-abiding citizens."[7] (He would again emphasize the need for citizens to obey democratically formulated laws after the Dakota War.)

News of Fort Sumter's fall reached Washington during a visit there by Governor Ramsey. He seized the initiative and went to the secretary of war, Simon Cameron, becoming the first state executive to offer to raise troops. As a result, the First Minnesota Volunteer Infantry Regiment mustered shortly at Fort Snelling.[8] Whipple rode up to visit them on Sunday, May 12, 1861. He preached to the men, newly under arms, and later described the occasion as "one of the most solemn services of my life." It proved a poignant encounter. Whipple recognized many of the enlistees as men he had seen either in the pews or on the streets of Minnesota's small towns. He was realistic enough about what destruction they might face to consider the occasion the last on which he could "tell them of the love of Jesus Christ." His words seemed to move his audience: the soldiers elected him the regiment's chaplain, an honor Whipple had to decline.[9]

During the next year, Whipple's opinion of Lincoln rose considerably, a sweeping change in attitude that coincided with the clarity of Lincoln's commitment to saving the nation. When Whipple looked back on that time and his decision to approach Lincoln, he specifically cited as a hopeful quality in Lincoln that the president "had known something of Indian warfare in the Black Hawk War." Whipple had also begun to perceive Lincoln as a man of considerable humane depth.[10] Taken together, these qualities gave the bishop an opening with Lincoln to tell him about how appalled he found federal treatment of American Indians.

In referring to the Black Hawk War, Whipple brought up a conflict that had taken place almost exactly thirty years previous, in the late spring and early summer of 1832. The fighting, largely between state militia and Indians native to northern Illinois, cut a swath of destruction across northwestern Illinois and southwestern Wisconsin. The war ended a period of relative peace between whites and Native Americans in the states and territories north of the Ohio River.

Lincoln, when he took the oath of office as president on March 4, 1861, joined a select, if largely unheralded, group of chief executives: men who had taken part in wars against Indian tribes. Four among his fifteen predecessors held that distinction, beginning with George Washington. As an officer of the Virginia militia, Washington fought on the Appalachian frontier with Indians as both allies and opponents during the French and Indian War. Andrew Jackson, who became the sixth president, defeated the Upper Creek Indians at Horseshoe Bend, Alabama, during the War of 1812; a few years later, he made war on the Seminoles in northern Florida. Jackson's contemporary, William Henry Harrison, later elected as the eighth president, defeated the Shawnees and their allies in the Battle of Tippecanoe in Indiana. Zachary Taylor, a career military man elected as the twelfth president, also fought the Shawnees, later pursued Chief Black Hawk, and later still led the U.S. Army in the Second Seminole War. Two other men who would achieve political prominence served in the Black Hawk War: Winfield Scott, nominated by the Republican Party as its presidential candidate in 1856, and Jefferson Davis, the Confederate states' president.

Lincoln's military service was so slim as to be easily overlooked—had he not used it as a source of self-deprecating jokes in his political life and called attention to it in writing. Specific stories about his weeks of military service make intriguing reading in light of what came later, when as president he had to deal with life-and-death decisions arising from the Dakota War. In the spring of 1832, shortly after he had taken out papers to run for a seat in the Illinois state senate, Lincoln joined the state militia charged with pursuing Black Hawk, whose followers crossed the Mississippi into Illinois. Despite the brevity of his service, Lincoln encountered grim evidence of battle. He helped bury corpses of soldiers killed in the field and may have seen the scalps of white settlers hanging in an abandoned Indian village.

Arriving in Illinois a quarter century later, Whipple had no reason to learn the details of Lincoln's service. In 1857, the future president was a successful attorney whose travel around Illinois allowed him time to organize the state's Republican Party. Whipple read the newspapers (in Minnesota, when the

Civil War had begun, he asked friends to get him subscriptions to New York and Washington papers too) and so knew of Lincoln's political ascent. Those accounts would have included Lincoln's impressive political performance in the seven debates he held with Stephen Douglas in the 1858 Senate race. All were avidly covered by the press in Chicago and further afield, some newspapers including printed transcripts of the speeches.

After Whipple took up residence as Minnesota's bishop, he stayed in touch with his Chicago friends. He had enjoyed living in the city and it would be the point of transit for any travel he made east. At least twice, too, he had opportunities to read about Lincoln, descriptions of his life from Lincoln's own hand. In December 1859 and again in June 1860—before and after receiving the Republican presidential nomination—Lincoln wrote two short autobiographical essays, describing his family and personal histories, to be published in newspapers and reprinted where they might help introduce him to Republicans specifically and the electorate in general. Both essays revealed that Lincoln's life had intertwined with violent events involving American Indians. Lincoln wrote that he had grown up knowing that Indians had killed his grandfather, whose name he bore. He did not mention that his grandfather's death had turned his uncle—his father Thomas's older brother—into an unrepentant murderer of Indians, a man rabidly bent on avenging his father's death.

Of two Lincoln "autobiographies," the most thorough of these personal accounts—and the one most revealing of his political life—Lincoln gave to a journalist friend, John Scripps, who had it published in the *Chicago Press and Tribune* in 1860, after Lincoln's nomination for president. Scripps had asked before for an essay, but Lincoln had put him off.

When Lincoln finally obliged Scripps, he disclosed what his family and some of his friends knew, that he had lost his grandfather to an Indian attack. He also mentioned his service in the state militia during the Black Hawk War. The essay Lincoln wrote for Scripps followed one he had composed before Christmas the previous year for Jesse Fell, an Illinois Republican hoping to help generate publicity for Lincoln's presidential aspirations. It was initially published in Pennsylvania but came to be widely circulated among newspapers sympathetic to Republicans.[11] The piece was four paragraphs, in which Lincoln mentioned his grandfather's death in a bit more detail than he would later. "My paternal grandfather, Abraham Lincoln, emigrated from Rockingham County, Virginia, to Kentucky, about 1781 or 2, where, a year or two later, he was killed by Indians, not in battle, but by stealth, when he was laboring to open a farm in the forest." The phrase describing the circumstances of the senior Lincoln's death stands out: "not in battle, but by stealth." In the other essay, Lincoln says his grandfather "was killed by the Indians" and that he "left a widow, three sons, and two daughters."[12]

Even though his grandfather's death occurred nearly a quarter century before the future president's birth, it held a special place in Lincoln's mind. Not only did he include it in the two campaign autobiographies he wrote at a crucial period in his life but he also told a cousin that the incident had been deeply impressed on him as a boy. Their correspondence occurred in 1855, when Lincoln responded to a letter from a man identifying himself as Jesse Lincoln. The latter had written, asking if they might be related. Lincoln said they were, based on details Jesse Lincoln provided. "As you have supposed, I am the grandson of your uncle Abraham; and the story of his death by the Indians, and of Uncle Mordecai, then fourteen years old, killing one of the Indians, is the legend more strongly than all other imprinted upon my mind and memory."[13] Lincoln did not mention how deeply that incident shaped his uncle Mordecai, inclining him to a spirit of lethal revenge that was absent in his nephew.

To early travelers and settlers like the Lincolns, Kentucky in the early 1780s (still part of the Commonwealth of Virginia) seemed a place of abundance, rich both in game and sites for settlement. When the Revolutionary War ended, it became a magnet for restless Virginians. For more than a decade, the Lincoln family had lived in Rockingham County, west of the Blue Ridge Mountains, a region encompassing the northern Shenandoah Valley. Lincoln's great-grandfather John had moved his family there from Pennsylvania in 1768 and eventually gave his two adult sons some of his land. The first Abraham Lincoln served in the Virginia militia, enlisting in the war begun by the British governor, Lord Dunmore, against the powerful Shawnee Indians in 1774. The tribe, spread across southeastern Ohio, treated Kentucky as a hunting ground. The Shawnees effectively controlled the Ohio River, the thoroughfare to British claims south of the Great Lakes. During the American Revolution, the senior Abraham Lincoln became a militia captain, a position of responsibility, especially after the war with the British shifted to the southern colonies in the late 1770s.[14]

The first Abraham Lincoln barely waited for the war to draw to a close before taking his family west. Lord Cornwallis surrendered to George Washington at Yorktown, Virginia, in October 1781. With his wife and five children, Lincoln ventured out onto the dangerous Wilderness Road, a route Daniel Boone had hacked through the forest in 1775. The Shawnees and their allies, determined to maintain control over the region, often killed would-be settlers. Their fierce tenacity kept southern Ohio and northern and eastern Kentucky embroiled in a conflict that lasted nearly half a century, until the War of 1812.[15] The Lincolns risked the road for hundreds of miles, traveling far enough to reach Long Run Creek, on the outskirts of present-day Louisville. The family, aware of the dangers they faced, built themselves a stockade in which to live.

Their defensive strategy proved insufficient to protect their forty-two-year-old pioneer father. In May 1786, he fell victim to an attack by Indians who may have been Shawnees. As his grandson would later tell it, an Indian shot the senior Abraham while he stood out in the open with his sons, planting his fields. The incident contained more drama—and, for the boys, probably greater trauma—than the killing alone. Thomas Lincoln, at eight years old the youngest of the sons, stood close to his father when the latter fell. The boy froze, immobilized by terror and confusion. An Indian emerged from some trees nearby and came running directly at Thomas. As the historian Michael Burlingame writes: "As the Indian prepared to kidnap the lad, his older brother Mordecai dashed back to the family cabin, grabbed a rifle, aimed at the silver ornament dangling from the Indian's neck, and squeezed the trigger. Luckily for Thomas, his brother's aim was true, and the boy escaped harm, at least physically."[16]

In 1865, shortly after President Lincoln's assassination, William Herndon, Lincoln's former law partner in Springfield, Illinois, received a detailed account of the incident from Colonel Augustus Chapman. Herndon became an indefatigable collector of reminiscences about the president soon after his death. In hearing from Chapman, a resident of Charleston, Illinois, he received information from a man who had married into Lincoln's mother's family. Chapman, born in 1822, had married Harriet Hanks, the daughter of Lincoln's second cousin, Dennis Hanks, and Lincoln's stepsister, Sarah Elizabeth Johnston Hanks. Chapman told Herndon that Thomas had been helping his father, "putting up a fence to a new field," the morning the senior Lincoln died. Chapman added that the Indian who shot Thomas's father had actually advanced far enough to pick up Thomas, who had the presence of mind to implore the Indian not to kill him too. The boy might well have been carried off (as young Peter Doxtater was taken from his family in New

York State). "Just at this time," Chapman recalled, "the crack of a Rifle was heard [and] the Indian bounded high into the air and fell dead. . . . The Indian had been shot from the loft of the House" by Mordecai Lincoln, at what Chapman estimated was "a distance of 160 steps."[17]

Dennis Hanks, Chapman's father-in-law, provided more information to Herndon about the incident, indicating how the story circulated within Lincoln's extended family. In an interview with Herndon on June 13, 1865, in Chicago, Hanks said he "wished to state one fact" about the killing. Hanks wrote, "In Kentucky all men had to clear out their own field—cut down the trees—Split them into rails, &c., and in putting on the last rail—the 8th on the fence[—]one Indian who had secreted himself shot" the senior Abraham Lincoln. "Then the Indian ran out from the hiding place and caught Thomas—the father of Abraham," Hanks continued, adding that Mordecai "jumped over the fence—ran to the fort—shot the Indian through the [portholes] of the fort—the Indian dropt Thomas—ran and was followed by the blood the next day and found dead—In his flight he threw his gun in a treetop which was found." Mordecai, Hanks reported, said the Indian had a silver half-moon trinket on his upper chest and "he drew his beed [*sic*] on the Indian, that silver being the mark he shot at."[18]

The murder of his father seems to have left Mordecai Lincoln, then about sixteen years old, emotionally unbalanced. At least two of Herndon's sources told him that Mordecai developed a lifelong hatred of Indians. Chapman, writing at length to Herndon in September 1865 stated that "young Mord Lincoln Swore eternal vengeance on all Indians, an oath which he faithfully kept as he afterwards, during times of profound peace with the Indians, killed several of them[. I]n fact he invariably done so when he could without it being known that he was the person that done the deed."[19] The following year, Herndon collected a statement from William Clagett, who wanted to "relate what little I have gathered from people much older than myself." Clagett had grown up in Grayson County, Kentucky, near Mordecai Lincoln. "While Mordecai lived in Grayson County there came a few Indians through there and old Mordecai heard of them passing through mounted on his horse and took his Rifle gun on his Shoulder and followed on after the Indians and was gone Two days[. W]hen he returned he said he left one Lying in a sink hole for the Indians had killed his farther [*sic*] and he was determined to have satisfaction."[20] From these descriptions, Mordecai Lincoln fits the model of a literary character from the early nineteenth century. Samuel Monson was the creation of a successful short story writer, James Hall, best known for a work titled "The Indian Hater." The story describes a man whose family died in a frontier attack and who then made it his life's mission to wreak revenge on Native Americans.[21]

The murder of one's grandfather is an extraordinary family story with which to grow up. Abraham Lincoln learned early on that his direct ancestor, his father's father, whose name he bore, was killed "by stealth." He could surmise that a consequence of the death was his fatherless father growing up as he did, poor and without education. The younger Abraham's birth took place in a rural region in which violence was endemic and warfare between whites and Indians could still occur. Before he turned twenty-one, Lincoln moved twice with his family. The first move took place when he was seven; his parents left Kentucky for Pigeon Creek, Indiana, where his mother would die and his father would remarry. Lincoln later described the place as frequented by bears and other "wild animals."[22] He made no mention of Native Americans; by 1816, when the Lincolns arrived, the original owners of Indiana's southern counties had ceded the region through treaties.[23] For about fifty years the Wabash River region "had been at the center of a violent conflict" over who would control southern Indiana's destiny. After the War of 1812, it passed to "a white American sphere of influence."[24]

The Lincoln family's second move, to Illinois, occurred when Lincoln was just short of gaining his legal independence at age twenty-one. In choosing to go to central Illinois, the Lincolns crossed into a region on the north side of the Shelbyville Moraine, where the soil was richer and the land more valuable and therefore likely to attract ambitious farmers. The area held possibilities that never would have been realized in the rural Kentucky and Indiana settings Lincoln had left. "The counties north of the Shelbyville Moraine, with more taxable wealth, could support better schools, colleges, libraries, and similar intellectual agencies."[25] They would also benefit from the invention, in Illinois in 1837, of the steel plow.

Illinois attracted a steady influx of immigrants, whose diverse origins contributed to making the state more culturally pluralistic. The crudeness and cruelty that marked frontier society began to wane. When Illinois achieved statehood in 1818, three-quarters of residents came from the South, half of them from Kentucky and Tennessee. But the Erie Canal, opened in 1825, changed the state's demographics, shifting its center of gravity northward. Between 1820 and 1840, Illinois's population increased about eightfold, from 55,000 to 476,000. By then, the legislature, prompted by Lincoln, had moved the capital north from Vandalia to Springfield. The population nearly doubled over the next decade, to 851,000, and then doubled again to 1.7 million by 1860.

A denser population, fewer of who came from the rural border states, meant a change of social manners. The Lincoln who emerged from Indiana into Illinois brought with him a mixture of character traits, some of which would be vital assets to his political career, such as his ability to tell stories, share off-color jokes, and display physical strength in wrestling matches. Other elements of his personality would be less attractive, such as the bouts of melancholy to which he was subject. The traits that set him apart from the society of his early adulthood were his compassion and empathy toward other human beings and even animals. None of the stories about him are difficult to find; all made their way into the recollections of his contemporaries and many subsequent biographies. Lincoln, who had stopped drinking in his twenties, entered a region in which temperance was gaining ground and where the extremely rough fighting of the frontier was fading out. Stories told about Lincoln at this stage of his life in Illinois include a notably humane side. He saved his dog from drowning in an exceptionally cold river during the move to the new state in 1830. He helped a drunken man find shelter one winter night and so avoid possibly freezing to death. Lincoln's close friend Joshua Speed recalled Lincoln saving some birds that had fallen from a nest.[26]

At age twenty-three, Lincoln spent a little more than ten weeks in the Black Hawk War. He took part in no battles, but he encountered the gruesome evidence of intense violence; twice, he arrived at battlefields in time to be detailed to help bury the dead. Lincoln enlisted in a company of volunteers from Sangamon County, in central Illinois, on April 21, 1832.

Earlier that month, Black Hawk, a chief of the Sauk and Fox tribe, accompanied by more than six hundred followers from at least five different tribes, crossed the Mississippi into Illinois at Rock Island—his home until federal authorities had forced him out two years earlier. Black Hawk had never personally accepted a treaty negotiated twenty-eight years earlier, in which some Sauk chiefs agreed to sell their northwestern Illinois lands to William Henry Harrison for $2,234 and allowed the tribe to be displaced by the government to land west of the Mississippi. "My reason teaches me that land cannot be sold," the chief later wrote. "Nothing can be sold but such things as can be carried away."[27] The war that bore his name was not inevitable. After the chief and his band crossed the Mississippi into Illinois in April, he traveled into north-central Illinois. But unable to reach an alliance with other Indians in the region, he turned back to negotiate with the white soldiers pursuing him. The chief sent a party of men under a flag of truce to talk to Major Isaiah Stillman. The major's men instead attacked the Indians, some of whom escaped to warn Black Hawk. The latter, although outnumbered, challenged Stillman's force, which broke and ran.[28]

Black Hawk and his followers fought a dozen encounters over hundreds of miles of territory in northern Illinois and southeastern Wisconsin before turning northwest toward the Mississippi. Their attempt to recross the Mississippi, near its junction with the Bad Axe River, brought the conflict to an abrupt, horrific end, as the army—assisted by sharpshooters aboard a river steamer, the *Warrior*—massacred hundreds of fleeing Indians, including many women and children. For the second time in the war, Black Hawk sent men forward under a flag of truce to attempt negotiations, and for the second time, white soldiers fired on his peace delegates.[29] In a historic footnote made ironic by what would happen later in Minnesota, some Dakotas allied themselves with the United States in the conflict. Their warriors waited for Black Hawk's more athletic followers to swim to the Mississippi's west bank, where they killed them.

Lincoln had left the conflict by then; in all, he served in three different militia companies, the last of which disbanded when the fighting moved north, out of Illinois, in July. In the first company, he gained a distinction about which he would later write with satisfaction, when his fellow militiamen elected him captain in a two-way contest. His militia service also delayed his political career. Lincoln had announced his candidacy for a state legislative seat on March 15, barely a fortnight before Black Hawk crossed from Iowa into Illinois. The election was scheduled for the end of July. Absent from Sangamon County all but seven weeks during that time, Lincoln lost badly amidst a crowded field of candidates.

Lincoln might have gone home earlier. His first volunteer militia unit mustered out in late May, but he reenlisted in another as a private. (The man who signed Lincoln up then, Robert Anderson, would—three decades later—serve as commanding officer at Fort Sumter under its bombardment by Charleston cannon.) When that company was mustered out in June, Lincoln signed up for a final tour, again as a private.

His militia experience left Lincoln with jokes he could tell about himself during later political campaigns. Acknowledging his inexperience of actual battle, he said on the floor of Congress—in an 1848 political attack on the presidential candidate Democrat Lewis Cass—that he had nonetheless undergone "bloody struggles with the mosquitoes."[30]

Although Lincoln's company missed seeing battle, Lincoln and his fellow volunteers came upon its bloody detritus. Two days after the fighting, the company reached the battlefield at Old Man's Creek, where the battalion—under the command of Isaiah Stillman—had ingloriously collapsed and fled before Black Hawk's smaller force. Lincoln and his comrades helped bury eleven men. A veteran of Lincoln's company told Herndon in 1866 that "the dead was all scalped, some with heads cut off, Many with their throats cut and otherwise Barbourously Mutilated."[31] But Herndon's informant told him that the first encounter Lincoln's company had with Indians on the campaign was entirely peaceful—indeed, more than that; it was celebratory. The militia had marched west to the Mississippi spending a day and night camped near the river before they turned northeast to Dixon. While at their campsite, Herndon's informant said, "a considerable Body of Indians of the cherokee tribe came across the River from the Iowa side with the white flag Hoisted. . . . This was the first Indians we saw[. T]hey were verry friendly and gave us a general war Dance[. W]e in return gave them a sucker Ho down[. A]ll enjoyed the sport and It is safe to say no man enjoyed it better than Capt. Lincoln."[32]

A month later, on June 16, Lincoln arrived at a battlefield called Kellogg's Grove and once again joined in digging graves. This time, Lincoln left a direct record of his encounter with the dead. "I remember just how those men looked as we rode up the little hill where their camp was," he later wrote. "The red light of the morning sun was streaming upon them as they lay head toward us on the ground. And every man had a round red spot on the top of his head, about as big as a dollar where the redskins had taken his scalp." Yes, he found the scene "grotesque," but at the same time, he felt a keen awareness of the natural light. "The red sunlight seemed to paint everything all over."[33]

Lincoln also heard about—and may have seen evidence of—one of the more brutal incidents in the war, when a band largely comprised of Potawatomi Indians attacked a small settlement at a place called Indian Creek. The band targeted the home of a Kentuckian named William Davis, whose dislike of Indians made him a very difficult neighbor for the Potawatomis living nearby.[34] Royal Clary, who served under Captain Lincoln, reported three decades later that he had seen the results of the Indians' raid on the little settlement: "[T]he Indians: they had Killed Davis and Pettigrew family. . . . We Saw the Scalps they had taken—scalps of old women and children. This was near the Pottowatomy [*sic*] village—farming place. The Indians Scalped an old Grand Mother—Scalped her—hung her scalp on a ram rod—that it might be seen and aggravate the whites." In an eerie foreshadowing of the most provocative accusation that Minnesota whites would levy against the Dakotas in 1862, Clary also said a full-term fetus had been taken from one woman, killed and hung up at the massacre site. He recalled that "strong men wept at this—hard-hearted men cried."[35] (The editors of Herndon's papers doubt either Clary or Lincoln actually saw the site but "apparently did see the scalps that Clary describes at an abandoned Potawatomi village."[36])

Despite evidence of the violent death of whites, nothing indicates Lincoln indulged in Indian-hating. Rather, in recollections by former soldiers of the campaign, his name often turns up in reports of festive occasions, as it did in the "Ho down" with the visiting Cherokees. As one man told Herndon, "[W]e had a great deal of Sport, Especially of Nights foot Racing some horse, Racing, Jumping, telling anecdotes in which Lincoln Beat all, Keeping up a constant Laughter and good humor."[37]

Herndon interviewed Clary, who also recalled camp life during the war and participating in card games. But, Clary said, most of the militiamen were "generally to[o] tired and hungry to have sport and fun." Breaking that chain of thought while speaking with Herndon, he went on: "An Indian came into Camp or was Caught by Doct[or] Early's Company and our boys thought he was a spy—sprang up to our feet—was going to shoot the man—he had a line or certificate from Cass. Lincoln jumped between our men and Indian and said we must not shed his blood—that it must not be on our Skirts—some one thought Lincoln was a coward because he was not savage: he said if any one doubts my Courage Let him try it."[38] The "Cass" that Clary referred to was Lewis Cass, who had served until the previous year as territorial governor of Michigan, where the Indian presumably had received his pass. (By 1832, Cass had become Andrew Jackson's secretary of war. Dr. Jacob Early, a resident of Springfield, commanded the third Black Hawk War company in which Lincoln served.[39]) Clary, four years younger than Lincoln, served with Lincoln's company in the Black Hawk War and, at forty-eight, enlisted in the Union army.

In 1866, William Greene told Herndon that the Indian "who Lincoln protected came to our Camp at or near Henderson Creek," a sixty-five-mile watercourse that runs west from central Illinois to join the Mississippi River.[40] This was said during a follow-up to an interview—one of Greene's first—that Herndon had arranged the previous year on May 30. Greene first met Lincoln in 1831, after he had helped build a flatboat with Dennis Hanks for Denton Offut, a merchant in New Salem. Greene served with Lincoln in the Black Hawk War. "An old Indian Came to Camp and delivered himself up, showing us an old paper written by Lewis Cass, Stating that the Indian was a good and true man[.] Many of the men of the Army said 'we have come out to fight the Indians and by God we intend to do so.' Mr. Lincoln in the goodness and kindness and humanity and justice of his nature stood—got between the Indian and the outraged men—saying—'Men this must not be done—he must not be shot and killed by us.' Some of the men remarked—'The Indian is a damned Spy.' Still Lincoln stood between the Indian and the vengeance of the outraged soldiers—brave, good, and true. Some of the men said to Mr. Lincoln—'This is cowardly on your part Lincoln.' Lincoln remarked ['I]f any man thinks I am a coward let him test it,' rising to an unusual height. One of the Regiment made this reply to Mr. Lincoln's last remarks—'Lincoln—you are larger and heavier than we are.' 'This you can guard against—Choose your weapons,' replied Mr. Lincoln somewhat sourly. This soon put to silence quickly all Charges of the Cowardice of Lincoln. This is the first time or amongst the first times I ever saw Mr. Lincoln aroused. He was unusually kind, pleasant—good humored, taking any and all things. But this was too much for Lincoln. This hushed up at once all disputes about Lincoln's courage. I was through the Black Hawk war with Lincoln and can say no man was more Courageous, truly and manly so. No man had more moral courage. He would do justice to all though the heavens fell."[41]

Like Clary, Greene had a personal history with Lincoln. A native of Tennessee, he worked as a clerk in Offutt's store with Lincoln in 1831. He was one of the men who voted Lincoln captain in the war, and he went on to become a wealthy businessman in central Illinois.

Remarkable as the story of this incident is, it is credited by such distinguished Lincoln biographers as David Donald and Michael Burlingame.[42] At its bare minimum, it shows Lincoln would intervene to prevent a lynching. But of what other American president had it ever been said, "He risked his own life to save that of an innocent Indian"?

Four

The Dispossessed

NEWS OF THE DAKOTA ATTACK ON THE LOWER SIOUX Agency reached Bishop Whipple in Saint Paul as he returned, by way of the state capital, from his pastoral visit among the Ojibwes. From that moment through the next four months he remained a man in almost continual motion, taking on multiple duties—as a recruiter of militia, an organizer of a hospital for wounded civilians, a comforter of injured and dying soldiers, and a fund-raiser for frontier families displaced by the fighting. Traveling to Washington and New York, he also vigorously stepped up his work as an advocate for reforming federal relations with the Indians. If he discerned any contradiction between his various roles, he left no evidence of it. He had already publicly stated his view of his essential civic and theological missions two years previously and put it in pictorial form. In 1860, he had designed a seal for the Minnesota diocese. Its motto began with the word "peace": *Pax per sanguinem cruces*— "Peace through the blood of the cross," it read. Below the Christian symbol lay an Indian peace pipe and a broken tomahawk.[1]

Henry Hastings Sibley, one of the best-known men in Minnesota, approached Whipple in Saint Paul on August 20, to seek his help raising a body of fighting men. A Democrat who had served as Minnesota's first governor, Sibley, then age fifty-one, had been appointed that very day as the colonel in charge of state militia by his successor, Governor Alexander Ramsey. Sibley knew the land and the Dakotas, having lived in Minnesota for three decades, first working in the fur trade. As a frontier politician, he had played a critical role in establishing Minnesota as a territory and later as a state. As reports of the war spread through the capital, Sibley asked Whipple to raise the alarm in Faribault, the bishop's adopted town and a center of population in the state's southeast. The Civil War having depleted the state of many of its young men, Sibley needed to construct an army out of those left behind, and he needed it done quickly.[2]

Whipple complied with alacrity. "I rode all night to Faribault," he later wrote, and reached the town—fifty miles distant from Saint Paul—as the sun broke over the prairie. He sighted a boy walking up a street, got him a bell to sound the alarm, then told the boy to shout out a message "to meet me in front of the hotel." A crowd gathered there, and Whipple broke the news about the war, repeating Sibley's plea for volunteers and taking down the names of all who were willing to go. He especially asked for men with guns and horses. Whipple also sought out his friend, Alexander Faribault, the town's founder. Faribault, a businessman who had descended from a French fur trader father and a mother with Dakota ancestry, led the little column of volunteers west. That morning, the bishop said, "they were on their way to join Sibley."[3]

Whipple did not go with them. (Not that it was unheard of for a man of his ecclesiastical rank to pursue a martial calling. Fourteen months earlier, Leonidas Polk, Episcopal bishop of Louisiana, accepted a commission as a major general in the Confederate army.) In keeping with his essential character, Whipple turned to a humanitarian mission. With his wife Cornelia accompanying him, he hitched up Bashaw for another long ride and drove his wagon forty miles west to Saint Peter, on the Minnesota River. The little city stood within a day's ride of the Dakota War's worst violence and had come to serve as both a staging area for militia heading west and a destination for refugees fleeing east from the conflict. Families—some with wounded relatives—crowded into the town, seeking safety or preparing to push on. It was to them the Whipples went.[4]

In the meantime, Governor Ramsey became increasingly worried about reports of the settlers' exodus from southwestern Minnesota, and he did not hesitate to pass his anxiety on to Washington. His state was threatened by an internal collapse, as its farmers and townspeople uprooted themselves and took flight. Thousands of people faced instant impoverishment, their crops abandoned, their livestock left to die. Ramsey wired federal officials no fewer than three times in the war's first week, pleading for help. "The panic among the people has depopulated whole counties," he reported to Secretary of War Edwin Stanton (who had replaced his fellow Pennsylvanian Simon Cameron in that office). The governor sent another telegram, dire in tone, directly to Lincoln. "Half the population of the State are fugitives," he declared. "No one not here can conceive the panic in the State."[5] His words reflected the raw fear that descended on individual farming families in the regions under attack. A Minnesotan named Electa Currier, who fled sixty miles from her homestead to Eden Prairie, near Saint Paul, recounted how her family had received a warning of an impending attack. After turning out their pigs to forage in the wild, they left the home without taking any possessions. "There were two of our neighbors' houses burned and two of our near neighbors killed," Currier wrote a relative. "No tongue can tell, no pen can describe the awful depredations, the horrible savages have committed."[6]

In Saint Peter, Whipple, Cornelia, and several local women attended to an immediate need by organizing a hospital in the county courthouse. The bishop found many refugees badly hurt by gunshots, hatchet blows, and other wounds. Fortunately, he and Cornelia could count on aid from Asa Daniels, the former government physician. Whipple knew Daniels and his brother Jared, who had also served as a government medical man during Democratic administrations. Deeply moved by their attachment to the Dakotas, the bishop had written on their behalf in February 1861, asking the next secretary of the interior (as yet unnamed) to disregard the spoils system and keep the men on the job for their merit. His letter went unheeded.[7] Asa Daniels, who years ago had personally cared for a wounded Little Crow, worked through those days in Saint Peter tending to injured settlers. Whipple followed in his stead, in the role of medical assistant, with needle and thread. Daniels, the bishop said, "set the fractured limbs and performed amputations while I sewed up wounds."[8] His work in the makeshift hospital put the bishop into face-to-face contact with the refugees in their suffering. (The experience inspired him to organize in the autumn a committee of wealthy business friends in New York to manage and distribute humanitarian relief funds that Whipple himself would raise.) He also worked under the gnawing fear that friends he had made among the Dakotas, especially those who had undergone conversion, might have perished in the fighting, as early targets of the war party.

At one point, Whipple's skills appear to have slipped and he injured one of his hands, which produced an infection that persisted for weeks and hindered his ability to manage his usual prodigious correspondence. Cornelia picked up some of his correspondence while he nursed his hand, and she gave voice to their anxiety. In a letter to a daughter, she worried that Little Crow and his allies "had killed all the people we visited when we were up there only a few weeks ago." Cornelia Whipple also felt the heat of the ever-growing anger toward Native Americans taking hold among townspeople and refugees alike. "The whites," she wrote, "say that no Indian shall live in Minnesota. They will shoot every blanketed Indian they come to."[9] As for the bishop, he later noted that in volunteering as Daniels's assistant, he won some grudging respect from the refugees passing through the hospital. Some of the afflicted thanked Whipple for his help, which, he said, "saved me from the hatred which border people felt for an Indian sympathizer."[10]

Two statements by the Whipples—about whites' lethal intentions toward "blanketed" Dakotas and the bishop being identified as "an Indian sympathizer"—deserve fuller examination. Whipple knew he would be called an "Indian sympathizer," or worse, during and after the Dakota War, but his experience in the hospital ensured that he did not lose sight of the trauma endured by whites attacked by Little Crow's band. He expressed his feelings in letters, both public and private. At the same time, he began assembling arguments for a statewide appeal that white Minnesotans consider rationally why the war had broken out in the first place. His message, he said later, provoked "bitter abuse" against him. But it also demonstrated his innate empathy toward an abruptly marginalized people and his faith in his ability to use logic and reason to persuade others to share his perspective.

As for her reference to "blanketed" Dakotas, Cornelia Whipple had used a shorthand term that itself pointed to a dangerous division that had grown between the Dakotas on their reservation as a result of influence by the federal government and missionaries working there. In the late 1850s, a minority of Dakotas began to move toward embracing the outward elements of the white settlers' culture. They took up agriculture, dressed like white farmers, and a few even converted to Christianity. Before the war, they constituted a distinct minority among the larger Dakota population, but they found strong encouragement from Joseph Brown, the federal Indian agent under President James Buchanan, Lincoln's predecessor. Small in numbers, they nonetheless stood out. They lived in houses and kept gardens; the men wore pants and shirts, and they cut their hair. The women adopted long dresses, like their white counterparts. This shift in manners and appearance caused deep unease among many traditionalists, not least Little Crow. Whites called them "farmer Indians" and distinguished them from "blanket Indians," the traditionalists. The latter had their own derogatory term for these Dakotas, calling them "cut-hairs." By either name, they numbered about four hundred (more than 10 percent of the reservation's population) by the estimate of James Lynd, the amateur anthropologist who died in Myrick's store. With few exceptions, they did not join in the Dakota War.[11]

The city of Saint Peter not only served as a way station for refugees and wounded white settlers but, in the story of the war, it also held a symbolic identity as the settlement closest to the site of a significant treaty-signing between government officials and Dakota leaders. In a meadow a mile north of Saint Peter, federal and territorial officials negotiated the 1851 agreement that cost the Dakotas nearly all their remaining lands. The treaty's consequences—alienating the Dakotas from their declining hunting economy and forcing them into dependence on uncertain federal benefits—became the long-term, precipitant factor in the war. (Saint Peter, founded shortly after the treaty, became a development project for investors who envisioned creating a new capital. Their vision, of course, involved the dispossession of the Dakotas.)

The treaty site—acres of bucolic prairie fronting a tree-shaded riverbank—lies adjacent to a shallow ford in the Minnesota River. As a historic crossing point for the Indians, the site was named Traverse des Sioux by French traders, and for generations it served as a rendezvous point for the native sale of furs to French and American buyers. By mid-century, the site had also become a station for Protestant missionaries.

The 1851 treaty was decisive in the development of Minnesota, itself part of a much larger expansion of the United States. How that development fit into the larger, national picture took shape during and just after the administration of President James Polk, between 1845 and 1849. In those years, the United States acquired independent Texas, went to war with Mexico, and negotiated with the British the American-Canadian boundary in the Pacific Northwest. Together, the actions put more than one million square miles under the Stars and Stripes. It was during this period that John O'Sullivan, a young journalist writing in New York, coined an enduring, popular phrase, positing that the nation had "a manifest destiny to overspread and possess the continent which Providence has given us." Coincident with this expansion, Congress also voted to admit to statehood Iowa in 1846 and Wisconsin in 1848, completing the political organization of the lands to the south and east of Minnesota. In 1848, a convention held within land already ceded by the Dakotas a decade earlier—a broad tract of what is now southeastern Minnesota—elected Sibley to represent the area in Congress. Collaborating with the politically influential Illinois senator Stephen Douglas, Sibley helped persuade Washington to establish a Minnesota Territory the following March. The same month, President Zachary Taylor appointed Alexander Ramsey as the new territory's first governor. Minnesota's white population was very small—little more than four thousand—and located principally around Saint Paul, in the shadow of Fort Snelling. Almost directly across the river sat Kaposia, Little Crow's village, and beyond it the enormous tract that a Saint Paul newspaper called "the Suland," home to the four bands of the Santee Dakotas. Were Minnesota ever to attract settlers, Ramsey declared in a speech in the capital, the territory must acquire the Dakota lands, which could be put to the plow.[12]

After discussions in Washington opened the way for Ramsey to negotiate with the Dakotas, he boarded a steamboat in Saint

Paul for the journey to Traverse des Sioux. With Sibley's aid, he secured the partnership of Luke Lea, federal commissioner of Indian affairs. Ramsey and Lea directed the treaty talks with four Dakota bands, first with the Sissetons and Wahpekons at Traverse des Sioux—the Dakota bands who lived further west in Minnesota—and second, at Mendota, with the Mdewakantons and Wahpekutes—the eastern bands living closest to white settlements.[13] Problems with the weather and late arrivals by some Dakotas delayed the Traverse des Sioux talks, but by July 18, more than a thousand Sissetons and Wahpekons had camped at the site. Lea appealed to the Indians with the argument that a treaty would benefit them economically, replacing their dependence on diminishing animal populations with a steady income from the government. He promised that Washington would provide an annuity, create farms, build schools, and set up clinics. An effective pitchman, Lea described the proposal as having been used among other tribes and had resulted in great success. "There are many other tribes of red men, who, like yourselves, once owned a large country—it was of no use to them, and they were poor; so they sold out to the Great Father, receiving goods, provisions, and money, with many other substantial benefits," Lea said. "Those tribes are now happier and more comfortable, and every year growing richer and richer. We hear of no starving among them. They always have plenty to eat and enough to clothe them."[14] One chief objected, staging an abortive walkout on the talks, but he returned shortly and the negotiations moved swiftly from there. A showy signing ceremony took place July 23. Ramsey and Lea then moved downriver to Mendota, where they had arranged to meet the Mdewakantons and Wahpekutes. Both bands signed on August 5.

The agreements committed the federal government to pay about three million dollars for twenty-four million acres of land, a swathe of prairie and woodland nearly equal to the southern half of Minnesota. The treaties specified the money be paid out as an annuity, with special care that it would go to food, clothing, farm animals, agricultural tools, and schools. They also called for a reservation for the four bands, a narrow knife-blade of land extending one hundred miles along both banks of the Minnesota River. Ten miles wide on either side, the reservation would run from Big Stone Lake in the west to a point just north of a watercourse called Cottonwood Creek. The treaty ceremonies included one flagrantly dishonest move, in which the Dakota chiefs were directed to sign another paper—for which no white present provided an explanation or translation—that bound the bands into an indebted relationship with the white traders who worked among them. The "traders' paper" called for the Indians to satisfy claims by these white businessmen for goods the Dakotas had purchased on credit.[15]

The Dakotas would later say they had no idea they had signed away part of their payments. The deception created an animosity that complicated future dealings with the government. And even though the vast land was not to be opened to white settlement for at least three years, immigrants swept into the territory, pressing close around Dakota settlements. By 1853, the *Saint Paul Pioneer* reported, "A great many people, hundreds, are living now in the Indian country, making all sorts of improvements, including expensive mills. Settlers are pouring in every day, and will continue to do so; for the government could not, if it would, shut out the swarming millions of our countrymen, for a distance of many hundred miles of country treated for, of which the river is the boundary."[16]

Little Crow attended the treaty negotiations at Traverse des Sioux and shortly thereafter signed the document presented at Mendota on behalf of his Mdewakanton village. At Traverse des Sioux, he met a traveling artist named Frank Mayer, on a western tour from his native Baltimore. The chief impressed the twenty-three-year-old Mayer; in his diary he wrote, "The chief is a man of about forty-five years of age and of a very determined and ambitious nature, but withal exceedingly gentle and dignified in his deportment. His face is full of intelligence when he is in conversation and his whole bearing is that of a gentleman." Mayer waxed enthusiastic about Little Crow's village. "I have seldom met with the same number of persons taken promiscuously from the ranks of civilized life who possessed so much politeness, gentlemanly feeling, and kindliness of manner as the Kaposia Indians."[17]

Mayer persuaded Little Crow to pose for him and rendered in pencil perhaps the finest portrait made of the chief, who dressed with great care for the sitting. "His headdress was particularly rich," Mayer wrote. "[A] tiara or diadem of rich work rested on his forehead and a profusion of weasel tails fell from this to his back and shoulders. Two small buffalo horns emerged on either side from this whiteness and ribbons and a singular ornament of strings of buckskin tied in knots and colored gaily depended from his head to his shoulders and chest."[18]

After the Dakota War began, neither Little Crow nor any other band of Dakota soldiers made it as far east as Saint Peter, but the surprise with which the Dakotas had taken the Lower Sioux Agency and the total defeat they inflicted on Captain John Marsh's command briefly raised the possibility on both sides that they might possess the speed and determination to sweep down the Minnesota River Valley, pressing on through its various towns and driving whites before them. Optimism worked against the attackers, though, giving them a sense of power in their initial surprise attack that would prove illusory.

During the debate that had raged within Little Crow's house over whether to go to war in the first place, he had accurately predicted how the conflict would ultimately go. His prophetic words must have seemed erroneous to the Indians who took up weapons against white settlers and soldiers that August day in 1862. Twice in a single morning, they had swept aside the authority of the U.S. government, taking the Lower Sioux Agency and then decimating Marsh's relief column. It was as the whites' own newspapers had appeared to report: the government was weak, incapable of defending itself and its citizens. But the warring Dakotas' resources were limited to the number of men on whom they could call. Lynd, in a good position to make such an estimate, had counted barely more than eighteen hundred Mdewakantons of all ages in 1858, divided between six villages. Passing Hail, a chief in the second largest of those villages, did not join in the war. Little Crow's soldiers included members of other Dakota bands, but they did not have all the Mdewakantons with them. Even that band was divided.[19]

As the Dakota War enveloped southwestern Minnesota in August and September 1862, the fighting passed through phases. The first, during the war's initial week, involved surprise attacks on civilians and accounted for many of the casualties among white settlers. Entire families perished in their cabins or fields, or on the open roads. Dakota soldiers took scores of women and children captive. A second, overlapping phase began Tuesday, August 19, and lasted eight days. In this instance, the Dakota attacks grew far more ambitious, focused principally along a twenty-mile strip of the Minnesota River in Brown and Nicollet counties, targeting Fort Ridgely and the town of New Ulm, which contained nearly a thousand residents, a substantial settlement in the state's south.

Dakota soldiers reached their military limits early when they failed to take either Fort Ridgely or New Ulm. The fort's defense was a remarkable achievement. The fort lacked a stockade fence and consisted of about a dozen buildings (including log houses) backed against a ravine. Little Crow urged an attack on August 19, when its defenses were low. After Captain Marsh's death by drowning near the Lower Sioux Agency, command at the fort fell to Lieutenant Thomas Gere, a nineteen-year-old with less than a year's military service. At the time of the attack, Gere had a case of the mumps, but it helped his cause considerably that he did not face an opponent unified in its immediate aims. Dakota soldiers, despite Little Crow's advice, were more interested in taking New Ulm.[20]

Kenneth Carly, a historian of the war, estimates that about a hundred Dakota horsemen attacked the town in the middle of the afternoon on August 19, in a relatively brief engagement interrupted by a thunderstorm. That night, New Ulm received one hundred and twenty-five reinforcements, led by Charles Flandrau, a former Indian agent then serving as an associate justice on Minnesota's Supreme Court. Flandrau brought with him three physicians, including Asa Daniels before he returned to Saint Peter. The following day, civilian volunteers in New Ulm elected Flandrau their colonel, despite his lack of military experience.[21] It proved a wise decision.

Flandrau, a muscular, athletic frontiersman, wore his dark hair parted on the right and slicked down across his head, and he had a bushy goatee that reached to his collarbone. He won laurels as a military hero for organizing outnumbered civilians into a capable defense force and also burning buildings that might be used as strongpoints by Dakotas. "He burned in the faces of their owners one hundred twenty-five houses and stores," the *Saint Paul Pioneer* would later say. "No despot ever exercised more absolute power or was more implicitly obeyed."[22] But Flandrau was a more complicated character than those lines indicate. Like Whipple, he was a native New Yorker. A trained lawyer, he worked in private and public service, in the latter as a county district attorney. He grew close to the German immigrants settling New Ulm; as a public official, he naturalized them as American citizens. He also served as an Indian agent on the Dakota reservation in 1856 and 1857 and, like Whipple, he came to believe that Indians needed to be trained as farmers and given schools. He sent a subtle warning to the federal

Indian office in 1857 that the "hunting grounds of the Indians have been taken from them before they have had time to become fully domesticated on their reservations."[23]

Later, one volunteer under Flandrau offered a verbal portrait of New Ulm under attack. The author, W. H. Hazzard, a twenty-one-year-old farmer and former dry-goods salesman, took part in the town's defense. Originally from Delaware, he had moved to Minnesota in 1859. He went to Saint Peter on Wednesday, August 20, two days into the war and wrote that he and his brother Thomas "found the people greatly excited." Men openly carried guns in the streets; volunteers prepared to depart for the action. "Brother and I joined the Company and went to New Ulm, arriving there Thursday Morning. We found the town under Martial Colonel Flandrau in command. . . . Every Man that owned a gun, no matter what description, had it in his hand expecting an attack by the Indians at any time. Many Men were walking the Streets with pitch forks or axes any thing that they could use in defense. We were greeted with reports that the Indians were comeing in great force, Murdering and burning everything before them." The Hazzards assisted in burying sixteen people who had been killed in the first attack. They also came upon thirteen others hiding "in the high grass" outside town.[24]

The second attack against New Ulm began mid-morning on Saturday, August 23, with the Dakotas fanning out across the sharply rising ground southwest of town. Flandrau later wrote that the Indians "uttered a terrific yell and came down upon us like the wind."[25] Hazzard, positioned on city's western side, saw that "the Indians like so many Crows arose out of their hiding places and, with a yell and a charge upon our forces, they were repulsed and we held the ground and proved to them, although we were outnumbered, we had force enough to hold our town and so we did."[26] Later that day, another volunteer, Andrew Friend, recalled, some civilians investigating a building found the body of a Dakota man sprawled under one of the windows. They carried the dead man down to the street and scalped him. "I had the scalp," Friend wrote, "but some soldiers begged pieces of it from me that I only have a portion of it left."[27]

By the next day, the two sides had broken off the fight. Between them, a hundred and ninety houses and other buildings had been destroyed.[28] On Monday, the citizens of New Ulm abandoned the town, taking more than a hundred and fifty wagons and heading the thirty miles east to Mankato.

Five

A "War of Extermination"

BISHOP WHIPPLE CONSISTENTLY LAID THE BLAME FOR the Dakota War on the mistreatment the Indians received from the federal government, which neither protected them from lawless whites nor compensated them adequately for the sale of their lands. The latter amounted to a theft of their livelihood, in his view, because the Indians, deprived of the means of a traditional existence, now also lacked the money and tools to make the cultural transition he wished to see them make to farming and schools. His argument found only limited support, mainly from people interested in Christian missions. Among his fellow Minnesotans, it largely lost whatever traction it might have gained in the midst of the war. The bishop's appeal to reason and to a more generous consideration of the Indians' situation became increasingly difficult to hear amidst growing public rage and anti-Indian hysteria.

The war persuaded a growing number of white Minnesotans that they could not share the state with Indians. They began to demand the complete dispossession of the Dakotas, as Cornelia Whipple had noted in her letter. As the Indians' attacks spread beyond the western reaches of the Minnesota River, popular reaction descended ever deeper into raw outrage.

Bishop Whipple recognized the challenge the backlash posed to his commitment to Indian welfare. Even before the war, whites had not been shy about telling him his outreach to Minnesota's Indians was naïve, even useless. He had been called an "'enthusiastic tenderfoot,' whose eyes had not yet been opened to the fact that there were no good Indians save dead Indians."[1] Whipple's early critics perceived him as a novice when it came to the frontier; he lacked experience with Indian life that would harden him against any idea that Native Americans might be racial equals. Cyrus Aldrich, Minnesota's representative in Congress, replied in June 1862 to a letter from Whipple, telling the bishop that the state's Indians lived better than most other Native Americans, so his concerns for them were misplaced. Republican senator Morton Wilkinson, also responding to a Whipple letter, put his feelings more bluntly. Wilkinson wrote to the bishop that Indians were hopelessly benighted, adding, "I do not believe that the efforts to civilize or convert to Christianity an idle race of barbarians will ever succeed unless you first induce them to become industrious, prudent, and thrifty—and then you can easily educate and convert them. This is the reason why I think the missionary labors among the Indians have failed thus far to accomplish much good."[2]

To try to understand such flagrant prejudice, Whipple drew a comparison between whites who held the Indians in contempt and European visitors who disparaged America by focusing on poverty and slums. Both biases were based on fleeting encounters with very narrow realities, he said. "Travelers usually form their opinions of Indian character from the vagabonds of the border village or the railway stations, who have lost their manhood by contact with the worst elements of our own race. It would be as just for a foreigner to describe the character and habits of the American people from what he had seen in the slums of New York."[3] Whipple, who had traveled for his father on business to New York City in the 1840s, would likely have seen those

very slums, culminated in the degradation of Five Points, a gro-
tesquely overcrowded and dangerous neighborhood run by gangs
and troubled by frequent murders. (The neighborhood attracted
the attention and disgust of a visiting Charles Dickens, who
brought his literary scorn to bear on its description.)

Whipple would be neither the first nor the last American to come up hard against the rhetoric of men and women
who—despite being firmly in the majority—regard themselves
as victims and respond with fear and a clamor for the harshest
penalties against their opponents. Whipple fully recognized the
war's brutality; he used the word "massacre"—appropriately—to
describe at least its opening stages. But he stopped short of identifying the war as a stark and simply-told clash of civilization
and "savages." Nor did he succumb to the conspiracy thinking
that began to grip the frontier as the war went on. Terrifying
rumors took root—among military men and civilians alike—
that the Dakotas were party to a political agenda, in which their
goal was not simply to kill whites but, specifically, *Northern*
whites. To that end, some suspected the Indians of being Confederate pawns, under the influence of Southern spies. What
better way to put increased, destructive pressure on the United
States than to open an entirely new front in the West?[4]

Current historians have said that some groups of Dakota
soldiers, roaming the Minnesota River Valley in the first days
of the war, unleashed particularly brutal attacks against white
settlers. Women and children sometimes fell victim as well as
men. In some instances, the bodies of the dead were hacked
and mutilated.[5] Nevertheless, in some accounts, it can be very
difficult to distinguish between fact and rumor.

The downward trajectory of public discourse, driven by fear,
can be traced through letters exchanged among settlers and
through the statements of political and military leaders in Minnesota. Their rhetoric shows what Whipple came up against.
The language used against the Dakotas became increasingly ab-

solutist, particularly after the war had entered its second week. By September, some settlers began charging the Dakotas with a singularly appalling crime: infanticide. In so accusing the Indians, the letters' authors might describe the act in horrific detail, but they rarely identified the family so victimized or gave the location where the alleged killing had occurred. Nevertheless, these horror stories (perhaps the most accurate description of them) established a pattern. The atrocities alleged by some whites found their way into official military communications and even into conversations in Congress. A ready audience of public leaders seemed willing to believe them and conclude that maybe state and federal officials had never really understood the Indians, if the Indians could sink into a state of wartime terror.

Governor Ramsey and General John Pope, the latter dispatched to Minnesota by President Lincoln to help deal with the Dakota War, began demanding the Dakotas be wiped out. By contrast, Whipple stated that Dakota soldiers who had killed unarmed civilians should be brought to trial and shown the force of justice, but he publicly warned against the dangers of acting in a spirit of blind revenge.

Lincoln and his cabinet learned of the Dakota War only a day after news of its outbreak reached Saint Paul. On August 21, Governor Ramsey telegraphed Edwin Stanton, Lincoln's secretary of war, with a simple but urgent message: "The Sioux Indians on our western border have risen, and are murdering men, women, and children." Four days later, Ramsey telegraphed Stanton again, asking him to delay implementing plans to draft Minnesotans into the Union army. Ramsey needed men to try to restore order. Entire counties were emptying out, as their white populations took to the roads. On August 26, nine days into the war, Ramsey wired Lincoln, again asking that the draft be delayed at least a month. By now, he estimated that fully half of the state had fled their homes. By chance, John Nicolay, one of Lincoln's secretaries, had been traveling in Minnesota when the war erupted. On the 27th, Nicolay telegraphed the president, striking a note very similar to Ramsey's. "Thusfar, the massacre of innocent white settlers has been fearful. A wild panic prevails in nearly one-half of the State." That day, Lincoln replied to Ramsey, reassuring him that the federal armies would not draw more fighting men from Minnesota for the time being. "Attend to the Indians," Lincoln wrote. "If the draft cannot proceed, of course it will not proceed. Necessity knows no law."[6]

Adding to Minnesota officials' concerns, within days the Dakotas scored a tactical victory against Colonel Sibley on a patch of prairie near a ravine called Birch Coulee. The site lay a few miles northwest of the ruins of the Lower Sioux Agency. This was the beginning of the longest phase of the fighting, which pitted Sibley's command against Little Crow and his allies.

On August 31, responding to pleas from settlers, Sibley sent out a burial party of about a hundred and seventy men, under Major Joseph Brown, the former Indian agent whose family had been taken captive on the war's first day. By nightfall of September 1, the soldiers established camp at Birch Coulee after a day spent burying fifty-four corpses, including the bodies of traders at the agency and soldiers under Captain Marsh's command. Brown left his encampment poorly guarded; Dakotas surrounded it and surprised his men at dawn on September 2. The resulting fight lasted into the next morning, leaving thirteen soldiers dead and forty-seven wounded, four of them mortally. The Indians lifted the siege only with the arrival from Fort Ridgely of Colonel Sibley, accompanied by several hundred men.[7]

The same day, Little Crow's soldiers attacked a volunteer company well to the north of Birch Coulee, near Acton, site of the murders that precipitated the war. Then the band attacked Forest City, a larger community in Meeker County, though the citizens there had put up a defensive log fortification against just such a possibility.[8] Not far away, residents in Saint Cloud built three forts, one of them a tower cut with ports out of which sharpshooters could fire.

Rebecca MacAlmond, an adolescent living with her parents in Hutchinson, southeast of Acton, already knew about the five murders that had taken place on August 17. Writing the next day, she told her diary, "Great excitement on account of it." By Tuesday, her family knew about the attack on the Lower Sioux Agency. From then on, refugees from western Minnesota farms and villages began streaming through the neighborhood. By that week's end, local residents pitched in and build a fort, and the MacAlmonds began spending nights within its walls. Nothing much happened until September 3, when Captain Richard Strout's volunteers came in from the battle that had taken place at Acton that morning. "They had lost four men killed, and brought in about 15 wounded. Some of the men are wounded very badly," Rebecca wrote. "I spent all the afternoon in helping take care of them. Two of the men it is thought will not recover." The next day she woke to the news that Dakotas had entered the town. "I looked out of the post-holes and saw a number running around on a hill. One German came in wounded by them, but fortunately it is only a flesh wound. They have ransacked and burnt our houses, killed some horses. . . . But a number of Indians have been made to bite the dust. They are skulking all around us," she wrote, using a decidedly negative verb common in settlers' descriptions of Indians' warfare. Firing between Indians and the town's defenders continued back and forth throughout the day, ending only when a hundred and fifty soldiers appeared and drove off the attackers. By evening, a report had reached the fort that the bodies of a woman and two children had been found in a field nearby. "They are shot up horribly," Rebecca said.[9] In the meantime, in Blue Earth County to the south, Mary Anna Marston Hallock wrote that the citizens of Vernon had erected "a barricade," a job that she said took a day and a night. They had put it up "around the tavern on a little hill," with space enough to accommodate about eight hundred people. "Those who were disabled were put inside the house, and the remainder stayed outside."[10]

Whites used the word "massacre" almost from the war's start. Now, in letters, diaries, and newspaper editorials, it came paired with an insistence that the Dakotas in general must be made to pay dearly for the violence. Nicolay, writing to Stanton in late August, relayed his fear that "2,000 warriors are striking along a line of scattered frontier settlements of 200 miles, having already massacred several hundred whites." He repeated Ramsey's fear that a general exodus of settlers was underway, an economic as well as humanitarian disaster. Everywhere along the Minnesota frontier, whites were "leaving the harvest to waste in the field, as I have myself seen in neighborhoods where there is no danger," he wrote. Nicolay also worried about an opportunistic attack on the settlements from the Ojibwes, a hundred miles northwest of the city. A third tribe, the Ho-Chunks, or Winnebagos, who had been removed from Wisconsin and settled by the government on a reservation in south-central Minnesota, were "suspected of hostile intent," he said. Nicolay reserved his special bitterness for the Dakotas: "As against the Sioux, it must be a war of extermination."[11] His remark crossed a rhetorical Rubicon. Others soon followed with more rhetoric, including men, like himself, who had access to Lincoln.

No one can offer an accurate figure of how many people died in the Dakota War. Far more fled as refugees, temporarily or permanently abandoning land they had once viewed as precious. Ramsey estimated that thousands evacuated the most severely affected counties. Some stayed away weeks, others months. Some never returned. Estimates of the dead varied widely, especially as the weeks passed. Bodies, left on the prairie, decomposed and returned to the earth. Afterward, Whipple and Lincoln each separately used the number 800 as a rough estimate for the deaths among white settlers. In so doing, they came in well below some newspaper editors' estimates, which ran as high as 2,000. Perhaps the most painstaking attempt to count the dead would only be undertaken seventy years later, by a journalist, Marion Satterlee. Working in the 1930s, surveying records town by town and including military men killed, Satterlee calculated that 411 civilians died, along with 77 soldiers. He made no attempt to count Dakotas dead.[12]

Whipple, as noted, described the war, during and afterward, with greater restraint. He made no use of the atrocity stories often accepted—and repeated—as facts that others cited. Many whites attributed the violence to the Indians' nature. By contrast, the bishop continued to blame the government corruption and mistreatment of the Indians, and he publicly told the stories of Dakotas who had risked their lives to rescue whites. His narrative was a lonely one, cutting against the grain of the dominant story. He persisted in telling it, without apology, while also showing his sympathy for the suffering of white civilians. Given the extremity of the circumstances, publicly following the path he did meant risking his reputation and even his physical well-being. On at least one occasion, a friend of the bishop's overheard a group of men planning to assault him. The friend talked them out of it, but he also let Whipple know.[13]

In September, General John Pope reported for duty in Minnesota on Lincoln's orders to direct the federal effort to end the war. He spent less than a week in the state before he telegraphed the war department to report fields, farms, and villages destroyed. Pope, born within four weeks of Whipple, seemed the bishop's mirror image in temperament, at least during his first weeks in Minnesota. He saw calamity and feared a worse disaster. He urged meeting the Indians with all the force the state militia could bear. He reported to Washington that unarmed civilians of all ages had been killed, farmers had been dragged from their homes and scalped, women and girls had been taken captive. He feared—and voiced his fear—that the Northern states confronted a probability of having to fight another enemy on an entirely new front. No longer would the Union forces be contending with just the Confederates; some soldiers would have to be deployed into the West to face tribal insurrection. Writing to Secretary Stanton from Saint Paul on September 23, Pope reported that "all the frontiers of Minnesota to within a short distance of the Mississippi have been depopulated, large towns and villages abandoned, and the property and crops of more than 50,000 people totally abandoned." He predicted that unless "vigorous and powerful measures" were immediately taken against the Dakotas, whites would simply empty out of a vast area, depopulating their communities and farms in western Minnesota and the territories of Dakota and Nebraska. Like Nicolay, Pope feared the Ojibwes and the Winnebagos would shortly join the war. Worse, he envisioned a firestorm of Native American violence erupting, a war that would set the plains afire from the Mississippi to the Rockies. The "whole of the Indian tribes as far as the mountains are in motion," he said.[14]

Pope arrived in Minnesota with a military record blighted by recent disaster. A Kentucky native, he had been one of four army officers to accompany President-elect Lincoln to Washington in 1861, a man of the border states loyal to the Union. Early in the Civil War, he proved an able leader in the midwestern theater, driving off Confederate forces in Missouri and seizing a strategic Mississippi River island. But after Lincoln appointed him commander of the Army of Virginia in July 1862, the general issued a series of aggressive orders regarding Southern civilians. His General Order No. 7 stated, among other things, "If a soldier or legitimate follower of the army be fired upon from any house, the house shall be razed to the ground, and the inhabitants sent prisoners to the headquarters of this army. . . . Any persons detected in such outrages, either during the act or at any time afterward, shall be shot, without awaiting civil process."[15] He also made an impolitic statement to his soldiers whose command he had assumed, suggesting that they had been more used to retreating than pressing the fight. His arrogant tone served him poorly, especially after his forces suffered a resounding defeat by Robert E. Lee and Stonewall Jackson at the second Battle of Bull Run on August 28–30. Union forces took ten thousand casualties. Lincoln relieved him of his command, and a week later, he sent Pope to Minnesota. One can imagine the general as hurt and angry—and desiring an opportunity to restore his reputation.

The longer he remained in the North Star State, the rhetoric he used in communicating to Washington became more shrill. Writing to Stanton on September 23, Pope estimated the Dakotas had killed five hundred civilians and taken three hundred women and children captive. But perhaps thinking raw numbers did no justice to what people on the frontier actually said, he passed along the gist of the bloody tales: "The most horrible massacres have been committed; children nailed alive to trees and houses, women violated and then disemboweled. Everything that horrible ingenuity could devise. It will require a large force and much time to prevent everybody leaving the country, such is the condition of things."[16]

Still, Pope's estimate of civilian casualties was on the low end of what the Minnesota public was coming to believe. The number doubled, tripled, even quadrupled, as refugees fleeing east told of seeing mutilated corpses strewn along the roadside, burned beyond recognition in still-smoldering cabins, or lying sprawled in their cornfields. Justina Boelter, a twenty-eight-year-old Prussian immigrant, spent two months hiding in the woods and swampland near Beaver Creek, scavenging food, after a party of Dakotas raided her little community on that creek. Eventually discovered by soldiers, along with one of her small children, she was taken to Fort Ridgely, but not before the soldiers had sought the body of another child, who had died of starvation nearby. The *Saint Peter Tribune* reported on November 4, "No conception can figure the vast number which have been murdered, but it must far exceed the general estimate of the public. The foraging party that brought in Mrs. Boelter buried forty-seven bodies, and left unburied seventeen. It is our impression that nearer two thousand than one thousand have been massacred. Doubtless hundreds that have been slain, and left upon the surface, will never be found, as decomposition is nearly complete."[17]

Within the war, the earliest reports from settlers often reflected visceral panic at the Indian attacks. Refugees trekking hurriedly east over the plains brought stories of random killing, particularly of adults unarmed and utterly unprepared for violence. Children died, too, although many seemed to be taken captive, along with their mothers and adolescent girls. White settlers' stories began to incorporate ghastly tales of terrible brutality. They told of Dakotas slaughtering infants. Throughout many accounts, especially those written by women, runs a dark Victorian locution for gang rape: female captives were consigned to "a fate worse than death."

Civilians began sharing details of the war—some factual, some rumored. Little Crow and his compatriots brought the town of Hutchinson under attack on September 4. Rebecca MacAlmond reported afterward in her diary that she heard a woman and two children had been killed on the prairie outside town. She estimated that "about 100" men gathered to retrieve the bodies, which they found "shot up horribly." The tone she adopted for her entries began to change after townspeople brought in an infant's body. "Killed by the Indians," Rebecca wrote, adding that she believed the child's mother had been taken prisoner: "A worse fate than death awaits her." Later that month, soldiers went out in search of two local men who had disappeared and were suspected to have been killed. Rebecca reported that the pair's bodies, located and carried back to town, had been "horribly mutilated." A man named Cross, she wrote, "was shot eight times. His entire scalp is taken off, besides his face is horribly mangled. Mr. Sanborn was shot a number of times. His face is all cut up with a grub hoe. The Indians took part of his scalp."[18]

Some refugees fled further east. At least one family turned up in Saint Cloud within days of the attacks, nearly a hundred miles from the fighting. Sally Wood, writing to her brother Plumer Drake on August 26, said the couple, with their children and a team of oxen, had nothing to eat. "He started and left all his crops standing in the field in hopes to escape, but they were overtaken and his father and brother killed and he came on and left his father and brother on the ground dead." Wood looked at the attacks in the larger context of violence the nation then endured. "We thought it was bad enough to have our poor men killed off by the rebels, by the thousands, but when we come to be obliged to fortify against the savage Indian that is quite another thing."

Increasingly, as individual stories of killings reached people living beyond the main areas of action, the letters that white Minnesotans wrote reflected a growing revulsion toward the Dakotas, born of a willingness to believe their warriors capable of any outrage. Laura Swett, living in Clinton, Illinois, received a letter from her sister Eliza, written August 29, in which the Faribault resident wondered, "Our poor desolated state. What will become of it—this Indian war will prove its ruin." By the time of her writing, eleven days into the war, Faribault's small population had become swollen with farmers fleeing for their lives from the Minnesota River Valley. "Every mother's heart has palpitated with fear as she has read of the horrid tortures which the savages have inflicted upon little children before their parents' eyes—two children found alive nailed to the side of a house—others fastened to the ground by stakes driven through them. It is estimated that 200 women and children

have been carried into captivity. This is worse than death—
Little did I think when I was a child[, as] I studied the history
of the pilgrims and read of Indian wars, that I should live to see
the day when I should look fearfully around my own home for
the skulking of the savage foe."[19]

In a letter written September 12 to her brother-in-law,
Electa Currier, who had fled the state's southwest for the area
around Saint Paul, described the Dakotas as hiding in the grass
"like a snake." They disguised themselves by putting flowers
and grass in their hair, making themselves effectively invisible
to white soldiers. More than a thousand settlers had died, she
estimated. She said she had seen a child gashed seventeen times
by a tomahawk. "I tell you it is an awful thing to see their work."
Another woman, Mary Crowell, wrote, "If only I could scalp
one of their men."[20]

In the meantime, Pope complained of lacking able troops
and supplies. He also wired Sibley—the field commander leading the militia—with instructions to show no mercy to the Dakotas. "No treaty must be made with the Sioux, even should
the campaign against them be delayed until the summer," he
wrote, envisioning the war continuing into 1863. "If they desire
a council, let them come in, but seize Little Crow and all others
engaged in the late outrages . . . hold them prisoners until further orders from these headquarters. It is idle and wicked, in
view of the atrocious murders these Indians have committed, in
the face of treaties and without provocation, to make treaties or
talk about keeping faith with them. The horrible massacres of
women and children and the outrageous abuse of female prisoners, still alive, call for punishment beyond human power to
inflict."[21]

To make it clear what he expected, Pope added, "There will
be no peace in this region by virtue of treaties and Indian faith.
It is my purpose utterly to exterminate the Sioux if I have the
power to do so and even if it requires a campaign lasting the

whole of next year. Destroy everything belonging to them and force them out to the plains, unless, as I suggest, you can capture them. They are to be treated as maniacs or wild beasts, and by no means as people with whom treaties or compromises can be made." On September 9, Governor Ramsey publicly demanded the Dakotas be either exterminated or driven from the state.[22]

Despite the governor's public tone, it was a measure of their shared concern for Minnesota that Ramsey and Bishop Whipple maintained a cordial professional relationship. The bishop had long planned to travel to New York City on October 1 to attend the triennial General Convention—the governing body—of the Episcopal Church. He informed Ramsey that while in New York he would raise money to help the war refugees; he also told the governor he planned to travel to Washington too. Ramsey saw a possible opportunity in Whipple's Washington visit and asked the bishop to present the case for getting cavalry up to Minnesota to fight the Dakotas.[23] (Whipple had a savvy appreciation of politics that allowed him to get along with political figures like Ramsey. Before he turned to the ministry, Whipple worked as a campaign manager and aide to politicians in New York State.)

The Dakota War ended on September 23, when Sibley fought a final battle with Little Crow and his Dakota allies at Wood Lake. On a spot of prairie below the junction of the Minnesota and Yellow Medicine rivers, Little Crow made one last attempt to ambush Sibley. Militarily, the plan might have worked, but a few militiamen, out foraging without permission, inadvertently discovered the Indians before they could spring their trap. Little Crow's soldiers initiated a fight but fled before Sibley's artillery.

The battle proceeded haphazardly, with some soldiers retreating before the would-be ambush while others stood and fired. Sibley restored order among his ranks. He shortly noticed an effort by Dakota fighters to use a ravine to flank his troops and ordered five companies of soldiers, aided by a canon, to drive the Indians out. Sibley's forces confronted and stopped another Dakota assault on their left. The Indians withdrew. The battle had lasted two hours.[24] By October 8, Sibley's soldiers fully controlled the Dakota reservation. Already, the military had begun bringing nearly four hundred captive Indians to summary trials.

Among white settlers, a sense of enormous vulnerability persisted, expressed in words of persistent outrage. Rosanna Sturgis felt terribly insecure. Writing to her husband, William, then off in Montana, she said, "It would make your blood run cold to read the account of the way they have butchered the whites. I read of one case where they hamstringed a woman and dragged her along by the feet until she died. Another where they cut a woman open and took her child from her and throwed it in her face." Sturgis was certain that General Pope had every intention of dealing out the harshest punishment possible to the Indians: "wipe them off the face of the earth."[25]

Even in the absence of such appalling charges, the civilian deaths in the Dakota War furnished Minnesotans with ample fuel for outrage. In one notorious incident, fifteen people—nine of them children—died at an isolated settlement around the shores of Lake Shetek, in the state's isolated southwest. The killers, who had trapped the settlers in a marshland later named Slaughter Slough, included an Indian man previously well liked by the families who lived there.

Stories of the war, initially shared by whites through their letters, would soon be published in books, becoming a part of the historical record. In November 1863, fourteen months after the last shots had been fired, Charles Bryant published a five-hundred-page history of the war that included nine lengthy narratives by farmer family members who had lived through the worst of the violence. Their stories had been collected by a commission investigating survivors' monetary claims. Bryant had served as an attorney for the plaintiffs, and in his introduction to this section of his book, he stated that depredations by Dakota soldiers included "little ones *nailed alive* to the doors" of their family homes (italics in the original).[26]

Bryant's narrators included three women whose testimony often seems to dominate whites' accounts of the Dakota War: Lavina Eastlick, Justina Krieger, and Mary Schwandt. The three serve as reference points—Eastlick and Krieger because they were young mothers who survived terrible wounds and lost children in the attacks and Schwandt, an adolescent, because she had the luck of not being present at her family's murder but nonetheless ended up a captive. Two other girls had been taken into captivity with her; one died from her wounds.

Krieger and Schwandt typified the demography of the settlers killed in the early attacks. Both came from immigrant families and spoke German as their primary language. Latecomers to the frontier, they represented a group with whom the Dakotas had not established good relations. Eastlick represented the restless nineteenth-century farm families who moved from east to west, with various stops along the way. Born in 1833 in upstate New York, she grew up in Ohio, married, and moved with her husband, John, first to Illinois and then to Minnesota. Eventually, the couple settled with their five children in November 1861 on the shores of Lake Shetek, about thirty miles southwest of the Lower Sioux Agency. The family put up a house the next spring and planted crops. Through Eastlick's account—eventually fleshed out in a twenty-five-page, single-spaced autobiography— the attack on the small settlement around the lake, two days after the attack on the Lower Sioux Agency, became notorious for its brutality against women and children. But Eastlick's story also contained an appealing narrative of unexpected heroism, with one of her young sons carrying his smaller brother many miles to safety. That ending mitigated some of the raw violence.

Twenty-seven-year-old Justina Krieger, a native of Prussia,

had moved with her husband to a settlement called Beaver Creek, in Renville County, Minnesota, only eleven weeks before the war began. The creek, on the Minnesota River's north side, emptied into the river almost directly across from Little Crow's village, Kaposia. Krieger's story of survival proved particularly riveting because she managed to escape death on three separate occasions, the last while lying wounded in a wagon belonging to soldiers who came under prolonged attack at Birch Coulee. Krieger told the commission investigating financial claims after the war about an assault on German immigrant families and their attempt to flee to Fort Ridgley. She alleged atrocities, such as watching as a Dakota hacked off the leg of her young niece and seeing a cabin burned down, incinerating young children within.[27] In addition to telling her own story of escape, Krieger included in her narrative a terrible description of a claimed atrocity against other civilians. When some of her neighbors— the Schwandts—did not join the others in the flight from Beaver Creek, men were sent to investigate. They found the family dead, except for two children, both missing. The killings, in the war's context, would be unremarkable but for Krieger's description of the death of Caroline Waltz, the oldest daughter. "The daughter of Mr. Schwandt, *enceinte*, was cut open, as was learned afterward, the child taken alive from the mother, and nailed to a tree. . . . It struggled sometime after the nails were driven through it!" Krieger offered no source for her story. She did say that Caroline's brother, August, survived the attack on the family but, it would seem, barely. He "had been beaten by the Indians, until dead, as was supposed," she wrote.[28]

This story of extreme brutality, in all its details, may have provided the basis for others, who were not present at the attacks, to write with an inflammatory generality. A year after the war, Harriet Bishop McConkey, a one-time missionary teacher then living in Saint Paul, published her impressions of the war. Titled *Dakota War Whoop*, her book includes a chapter simply called "The Slaughter." "Women were tortured in every conceivable manner," she wrote. "Some, with infants in their arms, had their breasts cut off, others their toes, and some were hamstrung and dragged over the prairie til torn and mangled; from that alone they died." She also told of an incident whose principal theme was infanticide.[29]

Stories like McConkey's found their way into popular circulation even as the five-week-long war went on. They also turn up in narratives written afterward, which describe personal adventure, if not eyewitness accounts of atrocities. Mary Anna Marston Hallock, thirteen years old at the time of the war, wrote a vivid account of the flight of settlers across Blue Earth County, near the easternmost edge of the fighting. The fear she shared with the others is amply evident in her narrative, along with a desperation that prompts her to wonder why the young mothers among them fed their infants. "What were they feeding their babies for? Why didn't they let them die? Wouldn't it be better to lay them down among the fragrant leaves, as we had the little child that morning, than to be tortured to death?" She continued: "We had heard the story of the scout at Vernon: how they had found near New Ulm six little babies nailed to a fence, head downward, and left to die, a cruel nail through each hand and foot. Some were not dead yet." Vernon, in the southern center of Blue Earth County, is about thirty miles from New Ulm.[30]

The Schwandt story offers a ground zero in the war's various atrocity narratives. The Schwandts, immigrants from the state of Brandenburg, Germany, moved to the United States, first settling in Ripon, Wisconsin, in 1858. Four years later, in the early spring, they moved to Minnesota, traveling up the north side of the Minnesota River to settle beside a stream known as Sacred Heart Creek. At the time of the move, Mary Schwandt was fourteen years old, the second of five children. She had a nineteen-year-old sister, Caroline, who was married to John

Waltz and lived with the family, and three younger brothers, August, Frederick, and Christian, ages ten, six, and four.

What the various accounts agree on is this: On August 18, Mary was temporarily living a few miles away, working for a family named Reynolds, who kept an inn on the road between the Indian agencies. The Schwandts, at their house, came under attack. Only August survived, after being severely beaten, perhaps into unconsciousness.

Mary Schwandt got the news that her family had been attacked while she traveled toward New Ulm in a wagon driven by three men. Two other adolescent girls accompanied her in the wagon—Mattie Williams, a niece of the Reynolds family, and Mary Anderson, whose father worked as a government blacksmith. Stopping at a house along the way, they heard the news that the Dakotas had attacked the settlements at Beaver Creek and Sacred Heart. Schwandt, in her testimony to a commission the next year, related how their driver then made a fatal mistake. Instead of opting to follow the road along the river, he turned onto the open prairie.[31] About eight miles out, they encountered a large party of Indians—Schwandt estimated them at fifty—carrying "all sorts of goods and pictures, taken from the houses." Two ordered the group to halt, and in very short order, they killed the three men and took the girls captive, but not before badly wounding Anderson with a gunshot, as she tried to flee. Later, when the Indians had taken the girls to a village, Schwandt said she was taken from the wagon. "[O]ne of them laid his hands forcibly on me, when I screamed, and one of the fiends struck me on my mouth with his hand, causing the blood to flow very freely. They then took me out by force, to an unoccupied tepee, near the house and perpetrated the most horrible and nameless outrages on my person. These outrages were repeated at different times during my captivity."[32] Schwandt retold her story, at greater length and detail (although omitting any allusions to being raped, simply saying it "was a relief to avoid the subject"), in 1894. By then, she had been married nearly thirty years to a businessman, William Schmidt, and had had seven children.

Schwandt was among the large group of women and children—both white and mixed-blood—whose security was guaranteed by a substantial Dakota "peace party." At the war's end, the latter arranged their transfer to Sibley at a site that immediately came to be called Camp Release. She shortly journeyed to Saint Peter, where, she said, she learned "the particularity of the sad fate of my family." She did not describe what happened to them but told about her brother August being struck with a tomahawk, "left senseless for dead," then recovering and finding his way to Fort Ridgely, along with a German immigrant woman. In retelling the story, Schwandt made it abundantly clear that—three decades later—she still felt troubled by violent memories. "A third of a century almost has passed since the period of my great bereavement and of my captivity. The memory of that period, with all its hideous features, often rises before me, but I put it down."[33]

Six

Whipple's Dakota Allies and the War's End

WARFARE IS BY NATURE OFTEN CONFUSING TO ITS ground-level participants, the clichéd "smoke of battle" obscuring individual and group actions, even after the event. The Dakota War, begun with a surprise attack and then carried on in bloody acts great and small for five weeks, seems especially susceptible to being told in fragments. The darkness that settled over Minnesota's prairies—sometimes literally, with clouds of smoke from the burning of farmhouses and other buildings—was seldom dispersed by the incidental reports and rumors spread by refugees.

Bishop Whipple, for one, wrote later of feeling cut off from any real news "for weeks."[1] Eventually, he heard that during the initial attack on the Lower Sioux Agency, Little Crow's soldiers put the mission of Saint John to the torch and burned it to the ground. But he also joyfully learned that Samuel Hinman had survived, as had Emily West, along with the Dakotas who belonged to the small congregation. He heard, too, a touching story of remarkable, physical courage shown by one of the Dakota women he knew there. "At the time of the burning of the Mission House, the wife of Good Thunder crept in and seized the Bible from the altar, wrapped it in a surplice, and buried it in the forest. As soon as she was able to do so she sent the message to me."[2] That Bible had been designed to look impressive, a heavy, formal presentation copy given by a European aristocrat. Its savior had acted under the impression, Whipple discovered, that the book she saved from the flames was the only Bible in the world. That woman was Snana—a Dakota name that translated as "Tinkling." Whites knew her as Maggie. In a powerfully positive way, she complicated the story of the Schwandt family, described in the previous chapter. Maggie's interactions throughout the war with Mary Schwandt indicate how difficult it is to generalize about the acts committed by Dakotas on the prairies. The violence that rained down on southern Minnesota came mixed, as happens in times of war, with acts of radical kindness and generosity.

Historians of the war have pointed out that many Dakotas—especially outside the Mdewakanton band—had little or nothing to do with the fighting. Some opposed it from the start, and they became increasingly vocal as the war went on. More important, some Dakotas distinguished themselves by intervening to save whites, either individually or en masse. When Mary Schwandt retold her story in 1894, she laid considerable emphasis on the friendship she had developed with Snana, who lived then in Little Crow's camp. Schwandt came to feel an enormous gratitude toward the woman she called Maggie. "Maggie was one of the handsomest Indians I ever saw, and one of the best. She had been educated and was a Christian. She could speak English fluently (but never liked to), and she could read and write. . . . Maggie and her mother were both very kind to me, and Maggie could not have treated me more tenderly if I had been her daughter. Often and often she preserved me from danger, and sometimes, I think, she saved my life."[3]

Snana had been married in the mission church at the Lower

Sioux Agency. She had also recently lost her seven-year-old daughter to disease. She took Schwandt from her captor to replace the little girl. She later recounted her own story: "The reason why I wished to keep this girl was to have her in place of the one I lost. So I loved her and pitied her, and she was dear to me just the same as my own daughter."[4] To protect her from the possibility of danger, Snana made Mary wear Dakota dress and accompanied her day and night.

Both Snana and her husband, Andrew Good Thunder, were friendly with Whipple. The bishop had baptized them both before the war. He had also baptized their young daughter, called Lydia, at her christening. The child died of a fever shortly before the war's outbreak, but the girl lived long enough to refute a rumor—among some Dakotas—that her illness had arisen from her close proximity to the Ojibwe children enrolled in the Christian school that Whipple oversaw in Faribault, which Lydia attended. Snana's marriage to Good Thunder broke up in 1865, and she eventually remarried. Three decades later, she entered into correspondence with Mary Schwandt, and the two maintained a friendship until Snana's death. Their relationship, particularly during the war, illustrated Whipple's vision of a Christianity that could transcend race and ethnicity and forge a new community of believers.

It took time, but stories like Snana's made the complexities of the Dakota War more apparent. The incidents in which Dakotas saved whites cut against the racist stereotypes of bloodthirsty "savages," never to be trusted, people with whom whites could not expect to live side by side. But only a relatively few people—educated about the Dakotas and the decentralized relationships of the various bands, one to another—stood in a position to recognize the different factions within the Indian communities at the time of the war.

As the top military commander in the field, Henry Sibley had that perspective. He had long lived in Minnesota and knew many Dakotas personally. Still, those most likely to speak about the Dakotas who took charge of whites' safety were missionaries. Clergy in the field—and this included Whipple—tended to relate the lifesaving intervention by Native Americans directly to the latter's Christianization. Converts played a substantial role in rescuing vulnerable whites on the war's frontier. But not all who saved whites' lives were Christians: Emily West gave no indication she recognized as converts the Indians who spared her and the other woman escaping from the Lower Sioux Agency on August 18. She merely recorded them as telling her they thought her good for her being a missionary. In another instance, a personal friendship with a Dakota man spared the life of George Spencer, one of the very few white men who spent the entire war in captivity.

Short, dramatic narratives turn up in the correspondence of people who lived through the war, or by way of their descendants, recounting family stories years later. In 1937, Margareta Holl Hahn, then ninety years old, whose family had settled in Milford, a hamlet near New Ulm, told an interviewer that her family had befriended an elderly Dakota man some years before the war, offering him food in lean times. Thereafter, he visited them occasionally, often bringing wild duck or goose eggs, which Hahn's mother prepared as a meal for him. Margareta said she never learned his name, but the man came to the farm on the war's first day, shortly after the Holl parents had taken their wagon to New Ulm to pick up supplies. He gesticulated with great urgency, but not enough to make the children understand him. "At this time a farmer drove by in a wagon with his family, and the old Indian practically forced the Holl children into the wagon, and no doubt saving their lives by this act. This was the last time the Holls ever saw the Indian." Parents and children were reunited in New Ulm.[5]

Even Little Crow intervened to save the lives of captive whites from possible killers in his own camp. One was August Gluth, mentioned earlier, the young adolescent taken into Little Crow's village to tend to captured oxen. Some settlers, taken captive, later reported seeing divisions within Little Crow's camp playing out in ways they never could have expected—with the chief's critics bluntly telling him off. Nancy Winona McClure Huggan, who lived with her family about two miles from the Lower Sioux Agency, reported that Dakota soldiers killed several civilians very close to her house, and she heard one woman—whom she described as an Irish immigrant—screaming for help. "I ran to the door and called to a young Indian that was about to kill her and he let her go," Huggan later wrote. "This Indian worked for us at times. I heard that the woman got away all right."[6] Huggan, who was of mixed parentage, was taken captive and placed in Little Crow's village. Her release came at the insistence of her uncle, a Dakota named Adayamani, who faced down Little Crow. Her uncle, Huggan said, told Little Crow he would take his relatives from the camp. "I only want what belongs to me," he said, and added, "You think you are brave in killing these white people. You have surprised them; they were not prepared."[7]

Presbyterian missionary Stephen Riggs later translated a long narrative told to him by Paul Mazakutamani, a Dakota who had converted to Christianity half a dozen years before the war. Mazakutamani had asked the Dakota soldiers more than once to turn over their captives to him so he could see them safely returned to white authorities. "I will go with them to the white people," he said, recalling a speech he made. "Then, if you want to fight, when you see the white soldiers coming to fight, fight with them, but don't fight with women and children. Or stop fighting. The Americans are a great people. They have much land, powder, guns, and provisions." In the speech, he seemed to echo some of the words Little Crow himself spoke in the early morning of August 18.[8]

Whipple, in his early reports on the war, expressed thanks that few, if any, of the Dakotas he knew well around the Lower

Sioux Agency seemed to have taken part in the killing. That indicated to him that the religious teachings he brought to the frontier had forged a bond—of Christian to Christian—stronger than the chasms of history, culture, and race. It hardly mattered that the Episcopal mission's building at the agency had been destroyed. It could be rebuilt. When Whipple wrote his autobiography, with its chapter on the war, he reminded readers of the complexity of white–Indian relations that had prevailed. He called the violence a massacre in which hundreds lost their lives and more suffered terrible physical and psychological pain. But while he described the devastation, Whipple still gave over the majority of his chapter to accounts by four Native Americans who had intervened—at great risk to themselves—to save whites. The bishop told his readers they should not think of the Dakotas as a monolithic presence, seething with hostility. There were simply too many individual exceptions to make that stereotype work. The spirit of this same message is what Whipple took to Washington in mid-September 1862 and also told to his fellow Episcopal bishops when he met them in New York City in October.

Whipple felt this deeply enough that his collaborative relationship with the missionary James Breck, a resident of Minnesota for a decade, suffered. The early news of the war and the destruction of Saint John unnerved Breck, who told Whipple that the violence meant the end of Indian missions. Whipple—like Breck under great emotional stress—responded by weeping, but he recovered himself quickly and declared to Rev. Solon Manny, another Episcopal priest in Faribault, that Breck had to be wrong. The Christian mission to the Indians would go on, as soon as reasonably possible.[9]

Whipple found inspiration in the Dakota converts. Some he identified as farmer Indians, who had adopted agricultural lives and played a role in saving whites, especially in helping negotiate the safe transfer of captive women and children to Sibley at

Camp Release. As a temporary settlement, Camp Release had been established in the war's closing days at the reservation's northern end, not far from the Presbyterian mission at Lac Qui Parle. The Dakota convert Taopi served as the farmer Indians' "chief." During the war, he reported being closely watched by Little Crow's soldiers, but Taopi and half a dozen others managed to secretly exchange letters with Sibley, who instructed them to protect the captives. "By God's help we succeeded," Taopi later said, "and the bad men were foiled. The prisoners numbered one hundred whites and about one hundred and fifty of mixed blood. There were two hundred and fifty-five in all. Many of the Indians of the Farmers' band aided me in my undertaking."[10]

In another story that cheered Whipple, a Christian Indian named Lorenzo Lawrence (Towanetitonna) rescued the children of two families, one of their mothers, and his own wife and children by taking four canoes on a dangerous nighttime journey down the Minnesota River to Fort Ridgley. Along the way, in the deep darkness, one of the canoes collided with a downed tree, tossing a boy into the river. "I was behind and heard the boy struggling in the water, and hastened to bring my canoe up to the spot," Lawrence recalled. "I came almost by accident alongside of the body as he was finally sinking, and my wife reached down and drew him into the canoe. The women were crying and praying. I told them not to cry as they would be saved, but that I did not know what would become of me." Along the way, they passed the site of the ferry at the Lower Sioux Agency, and a bit farther along, Lawrence spotted a pale form in the water. Rowing closer, they discerned Captain Marsh's body, lying against a tree bough. The little party continued on to the fort, where Lawrence called out to a soldier on guard duty, identifying himself as an Indian and adding, "Come and see what I have brought." The next day, he led a party of soldiers to recover Marsh's body. "They promised to pay me for so doing, but I never received anything," Lawrence stated.[11]

Perhaps the single greatest rescue was accomplished by John Other Day (Anpetutokeca), a Christian Indian who lived near the Upper Sioux Agency. Over the course of discussions with his fellow Dakotas there, he came to believe that although none had been involved in the initial attacks at the Lower Sioux Agency, the situation was extremely volatile and dangerous. It would continue to deteriorate, as news came in of victories by Little Crow, which demoralized the Indians who did not want to fight. Other Day saw a crowd of young men, all armed and apparently waiting for some direction. "Just then, looking over the prairie, I saw a cloud of dust and soon heard the sound of horses' hoofs. I at once knew that it was the young men and warriors of White Lodge's Band coming to kill the whites and plunder the trading-posts. These were the most unruly Indians of the Upper Agency." Other Day first helped gather the whites into a brick building at the agency overnight. The next morning, he urged them to flee across the Minnesota River and over the prairie. Other Day went as their guide. After two full days on the prairie, he got them to safety. He had started with sixty-five, he recalled, but lost three German immigrants on the first day when they declared they would go reconnoiter the settlement at Beaver Creek. "I told them that so long as we continued together, we would be safe; but if we separated into small parties we would be in great danger if overtaken by Indians. The men were killed soon after leaving us."[12]

Through his knowledge of their testimonies, Whipple could incorporate personal accounts of people known to him and attempt to persuade whites that the war had been more complex than the racial struggle many described. Dakota men and women had played important roles in saving civilians. The bishop did not cherry-pick the overall narrative. He knew from his own, direct experience, as Asa Daniels's assistant during the days he had spent in Saint Peter, just how brutal some Dakota men had been against white civilians. He had seen the wounds, heard the stories of families wiped out. But he possessed a more nuanced view of the war and its causes, especially when he added that to his knowledge of the corruption that infested federal dealings with the Indians before the war.

Whipple was not alone in working to preserve a record of individual acts of friendship by the Dakotas. In the months following the war, a most unusual narrative was set forth by Sarah Wakefield, who had spent the war as a captive. She was the wife of the government-appointed doctor at the Upper Sioux Agency (who himself would be rescued by John Other Day). Wakefield and her two small children were captured on the war's first day as they attempted to escape in a horse-drawn wagon to Fort Ridgely. Their driver, a man named George Gleason, appeared to ignore the obvious evidence of grave danger in the smoke of burning buildings that rose through the otherwise clear skies that day. Based on her later description, he acted oddly that day, singing and laughing, until they came upon two armed Indians. One, a man named Hapa, shot down Gleason. The other, whom she knew as Chaska, saved her life, protecting her then from his friend and later over the course of the six weeks Wakefield and her children spent as captives in a Dakota village. Wakefield was a large woman, weighing by her account just over two hundred pounds at the time of her capture. She also described herself as essentially fearful; she suffered deep and frequent anxiety during her captivity, and her hair turned white. Hapa threatened her from time to time, as did other men, but she received support and protection from Chaska and, in his absence, several Dakota women in the camp.

Wakefield published her narrative, titled *Six Weeks in the Sioux Tepees*, a year after the war. By then, she had failed in her efforts to persuade the military commission that tried nearly four hundred Dakota War prisoners, including Chaska, that he was an honorable man, thoroughly deserving of his life and freedom. Her testimony instead earned her wide condemnation, mainly in the form of rumors that she had become sexually involved with Chaska during her captivity. She denied it, strenuously, in her book—and in so doing, she went a step further, telling her readers that Chaska was, in effect, a gentleman. "Very few Indians, or *even white men*, would have treated me in the manner he did," Wakefield wrote (italics hers). "I was in his power, and why did he not abuse me? Because he knew that it was a sin; he knew that I was a wife and he always intended to restore me to my husband."[13]

When Wakefield had originally arrived with her family at the Lower Sioux Agency in June 1861, she came down the Minnesota River aboard a steamboat, just when the Indians' annuity was to be paid out. Her first impression of the Dakotas was negative: those she met at the agency she thought "filthy, nasty, greasy."[14] But over the ensuing months, her attitude changed markedly. She did not study the situation with the conviction of Bishop Whipple, but she became convinced that the Dakotas were being ill treated—and that made some of them dangerous. She described the basic injustice of the annuity payments: "As soon as they receive it, the Traders surround them, saying, you owe me so much for flour. Another says, you owe me so much for sugar, &c., and the Indian gives it all up, never knowing whether it is right or not." She blamed "all the evil habits" she found among the Dakotas on the traders—alcohol abuse, the sexual misuse of women, and blasphemous cursing.[15]

Writing from the perspective of a year after the event, in the comfort of a family reunited, Wakefield recounted the fear she often felt in captivity, but more than that, her gratitude at the kindnesses she also experienced. She came through with her life and children. She wondered at the mistreatment the Dakotas suffered before the war, how they "bore so much and so long without retaliation." As for her own feelings, "I always felt as if they were God's creatures."[16]

Seven

To the Gates of Mercy

BISHOP WHIPPLE LEFT MINNESOTA ON HIS MOMEN-
tous trip east before the final battle between Colonel Sibley's
forces and Little Crow's soldiers took place at Wood Lake. Leaving the state at a time of continuing crisis amounted to a gamble
for Whipple, but the consequences of the trip—first to Washington, then to New York City—marked a major transition in
his life. He departed a frontier bishop with a regionally known
cause; he would return a far more widely known activist, confident he could seek out powerful men, secular and ecclesiastical,
to further his goal of combating corruption and abuse in federal
relations with Native American tribes. He would emerge from
the trip among the ranks of prominent nineteenth-century religious advocates of social reform—a progressive phalanx that
included exponents of women's rights, temperance laws, and
abolitionism.

The devastation wrought by the Dakota War simply increased Whipple's sense of urgency about his mission. He had
developed the conviction that he must take his message directly
to President Lincoln, but he also sought to rally his fellow Episcopal bishops to the cause—a formidable project, given that
the latter did not speak out on political issues. Officially, the

church took no position on slavery or against secession.

What helped Whipple in September 1862 was his ability to call directly on two important contacts in Washington. Both could aid him in getting to Lincoln. Weeks earlier, the president had appointed Henry Halleck, a cousin of Whipple's on his mother's side, as general-in-chief of Union forces. Halleck and Whipple had been close for years and regularly exchanged letters. As a soldier, Halleck had distinguished himself by having written a well-regarded textbook on military tactics; he also achieved success on the battlefield as a commander in the West. He would shortly prove himself incapable of the tough administrative job Lincoln had hoped he would do, but that disappointment still lay ahead at the time the bishop reached Washington. (Whipple's impending visit with Halleck excited Governor Ramsey, who implored him to try to "prevail upon General Halleck to send to this state as speedily as possible a regiment of cavalry."[1])

Through the Episcopal Church, the bishop also knew Salmon Chase, Lincoln's secretary of the treasury. Politically, the two men were unlike: Nearly fifteen years older than Whipple, Chase had become an ardent antislavery advocate in the 1830s and helped found the Republican Party. Chase was elected in 1856 as Ohio's governor. The two men had a deep, ecclesiastical connection. Born in New Hampshire, Chase left home at twelve to become a ward of his uncle, Rev. Philander Chase. The elder Chase became Ohio's, and later Illinois's, first Episcopal bishop and devoted his life to building up the church in the West—a predecessor whose work Whipple would naturally appreciate. In 1862, the younger Chase wrote Lincoln a warm message on his official Treasury calling card, endorsing Whipple. "Dear Sir, Bishop Whipple of the Episcopal Church of Minnesota desires some conversation with you; and knowing his great worth I take pleasure in introducing him."[2]

The bishop's visit to Washington, and his plan to enlist the

Episcopal Church's hierarchy in his campaign, represented his sixth attempt in thirty months to persuade federal officials to enact policy changes on behalf of the Indians. Whipple's efforts leading up to his sit-down meeting with Lincoln in the White House reveal the determination of a man not to be put off or disappointed, despite his being ignored and even insultingly rebuffed.

After he took up residence in Minnesota in February 1860, Whipple tried no fewer than three times to get the attention of President James Buchanan or his cabinet. Buchanan was a Pennsylvania Democrat whose political interests lay principally in foreign affairs. Whipple first forwarded to him a letter on Indian reform from John Dix, a prominent New York Democrat well known to the president. The bishop then wrote Buchanan directly on the subject, laying out his own ideas for reform. Buchanan never responded.

Whipple, fairly occupied with the business of running a new diocese, waited before making his next move. He had to devote considerable attention to the demands of being a frontier bishop. He oversaw a thin and scattered flock whose numbers and institutions he wanted to build up. Administrative demands on his time included personnel matters, making plans for new buildings, and responding to letters expressing the hopes and complaints of laypeople regarding their church. Early correspondence shows him thanking donors for gifts and exchanging letters with his priests about the relative vitality of their parishes. He had his share of headaches. A man falsely claiming to be a priest turned up in Minnesota and had to be revealed as a fraud and persuaded to leave the state. A woman complained about a cleric's flirtatious behavior, prompting Whipple to respond, "He was sent to Wabasha and while there complaints were made to me that at one time he was engaged to be married to two Ladies."[3]

In the fall of 1860, with Lincoln one of four candidates seeking the presidency, Whipple launched his first effort to lobby federal officials in person by going directly to Washington. Whipple kept up with the newspapers and so had ample opportunity to become familiar with Southern political rhetoric, but he was surprised by the blunt talk of secession he encountered. Before making the trip, the bishop obtained a letter of introduction from J. K. Sass, a friend and fellow Episcopalian. A prominent banker in Charleston, South Carolina, Sass felt enthusiasm for missionary work. He sympathized with Whipple's ideas about reforming the federal Indian system. To try to help, Sass wrote to a fellow Southerner he thought might draw Buchanan's attention to the matter. The letter led to a meeting with Sass's acquaintance, a person Whipple would later identify only as "a prominent Southern statesman." The bishop took to the meeting another Episcopal priest, a Southerner living in Washington, but almost from the start, the conversation went poorly. Sass's acquaintance frankly dismissed Whipple's concerns—on sectional grounds, as a Northern matter. He predicted Lincoln would be elected and then South Carolina would lead the other slaveholding states out of the Union. He dismissively told Whipple to wait until then. "You will have to seek justice for your Indians from the Northern Government," he said.[4] The man was likely to have been Jacob Thompson, Buchanan's secretary of the interior, whose office directly oversaw Indian relations. Thompson served a decade as a congressman from Mississippi, even chairing the House Committee on Indian Affairs. A pro-slavery member of Buchanan's cabinet, he would resign in January 1861 when Mississippi seceded from the Union. His words appalled the bishop. "Is it possible," Whipple asked, "that I hear a representative of the Government say that even its trusted servants are plotting for its destruction?" Whipple's companion—Rev. Charles Hall—responded just as angrily, effectively comparing secessionists with the biblical pharaoh whose heart God had "hardened" against allowing his Israelite slaves to leave Egypt. In the biblical story, disaster shortly befalls the Egyptians. "If you go out of the Union," Hall warned, "it will be because God has permitted you to be stone-blind, and slavery will be doomed. It will be a righteous retribution." Hall spoke as a prophet. Whipple remembered the miniature sermon, including it in his autobiography.[5]

On November 6, Lincoln triumphed in the election, receiving nearly 40 percent of the popular vote and an overwhelming victory in the electoral college, 180 votes to 143, the latter divided among the other three candidates, who included Stephen Douglas, running as the choice of mainstream Democrats. Lincoln carried not a single state in which slavery was legal. Six weeks later, the Union began to break up, first with South Carolina voting for secession.

Whipple, watching from Minnesota in anguish over the sectional crisis, continued to attempt to intervene in ways small and large on behalf of the Indians during the change in administrations. He challenged the spoils system, under which an incoming administration could legally turn out the occupants of federal offices and replace them with men of its own choice, regardless of their commitment or competence in their duties. On February 23, 1861, he wrote, appealing to John Dix, recently appointed secretary of the treasury by Buchanan, to help save the jobs of the brothers Asa and Jared Daniels, the physicians serving the Dakotas, whose work and commitment Whipple admired. Whipple described the Daniels brothers as "comparatively strangers to me," but added, "I have seen so much and heard so much of their kindness to the Indians, their skill and faithfulness, that it would indeed be a loss to lose them." Whipple asked Dix "to send this note to Gov. Seward or someone in the counsels of the new Administration with a line from yourself stating what you know of my effort." William Seward had served two terms as governor of New York, from 1838 to 1842, and would succeed Dix in the U.S. Senate in 1849, an office

Seward held until joining Lincoln's cabinet as secretary of state.[6]

The bishop, who typically penned several letters in a single sitting, also wrote the incoming secretary of the interior, whose office had direct authority over Indian affairs. Buchanan had not replaced Jacob Thompson after Thompson had resigned in January. The new secretary would be Caleb Blood Smith, an Indiana politician who had worked in Lincoln's presidential campaign, although Whipple did not yet know Smith would be chosen. On February 23, he wrote a "dear sir" letter, broadly pleading that whoever filled the job appoint the ablest men to positions responsible for the Indians' welfare. "Let men who seek political rewards go somewhere else," Whipple said, directly contradicting the idea of political patronage. Referring to those who would supervise Native American affairs at the local level, he said, "I pray you give them men of unswerving honesty, not to be bought or sold, men of heart, of love, men who will not fear to execute law. It would be better to find men who knew Indian character and have tact to influence it for good." Whipple also specifically asked for men "who fear God" or, at least, would not hinder missionary efforts to convert the Indians. Whipple could write with a concise boldness.[7]

Whipple had had enough experience of Washington and its agents in Minnesota by then to assume that whoever became the interior secretary, the supervisor of Indian affairs, and the federal agent at the Dakota reservation, it was unlikely any of these men would possess special expertise about Native Americans. So, drawing on his personal experience among Minnesota's Indians, he did his best to educate his reader. He devised a short and quite remarkable statement he used frequently thereafter, displaying his growing respect for the Indians as spiritual and moral beings. "The North American Indians are of the best of heathen uncivilized races. They are not idolators. They believe in a Great Spirit. They have home affections. They have strong national pride and love of country. They are generally chaste, truthful, honest, generous, and hospitable. If all this had been changed until degradation and poverty are stamped upon the race, it is a curse given to them by a Christian people."[8] To note that this represented a minority viewpoint on the frontier, or for that matter in Washington, is to recognize how deeply Whipple had been thinking about his experiences in a pluralistic society and engaging the idea that the duty of moral leadership demanded specific actions from him. In place of condescension, he argued for respect for native people, as persons possessed of an honorable culture.

The language he used marked him as an unusual nineteenth-century Christian missionary. Theologically, Whipple went about as far as a clergyman in a nationally influential church could go at the time, in finding positive attributes in a religious culture outside his own. Considering how many people in religious life did not share this same level of respect, and how many more showed not the least interest in Native Americans as a people, Whipple's statement is striking. It offers a foretaste of the direct appeals he would make in Minnesota after the Dakota War. It also shows him honing the arguments for justice that he would make to Lincoln in 1862.

Letters written by and to prominent people seldom stay private. Besides, Whipple repeatedly shared his convictions about the Indians with fellow Minnesotans, enough to put him in the crosshairs of public criticism long before the Dakota War. He seldom discussed the hostility he encountered, but, unsurprisingly, it could rankle, especially the charge that he neglected his duties among whites in the state. He described his anger in a reply he wrote to an admiring letter he received from a Rhode Island businessman in early 1862. The businessman had praised Whipple for his work among the Indians. The bishop responded with thanks: "I owe you all I have, my prayers and blessing. There is so much of a cold doubt and wicked neglect, cruel suspicions and slanders, that word of cheer is like music.

You would be pained if I told you half [of what] men have said because I believed Indians had souls—and could learn of Jesus. Perhaps this is too strong. I have been accused of neglecting my white field and wasting money on Indian Missions. I have preached since last June over two hundred sermons to white men. I have preached probably thirty times to Indians since my consecration." The bishop calculated the annual cost of keeping missionaries among the Dakotas and Ojibwes at about $1,500 a year. He added, "Thank God there are men who do not be-grudge the pittance."[9]

Despite Whipple's sensitivity to Native Americans, he chose a distinctly inauspicious time in which to resume his lobbying on their behalf and to try to introduce himself directly to President Lincoln. He wrote from Faribault on March 6, 1862, beginning, "Sir, I would not add a feather's weight to the heavy burdens of your heart." But, he continued, "I must plead to someone for my poor heathen wards who have no one else to plead for them. Where shall a Christian bishop look for justice, if not to you whom God has made the Chief Ruler of the nation?"[10]

What were those heavy burdens to which Whipple alluded? Above all, they included a divided Union engaged in an escalat-ing Civil War. But the letter's date suggests Whipple was aware of the enormous personal tragedy that had just befallen Lincoln in the White House. On February 20, William Wallace Lincoln (known to his parents and brothers as "Willie") died after an agonizing bout with typhoid fever. He was twelve. The same illness also sickened but did not kill his younger brother Tad. Abraham and Mary Lincoln had already lost one other of their four sons to illness: Eddy, who had died in February 1850. Willie had been born about nine months later and had filled a hole in the family's life. By many accounts, Willie was his father's fa-vorite; his death drove Lincoln into a time of mourning distin-guished by a grief he made no attempt to hide. Only by early March had he sufficiently recovered to resume his full duties.

By then, too, he had begun discussing possible ways in which the federal government might help end slavery.[11] The devastating family crisis; the new focus on the problem of slavery; the Union's uncertain military situation, with General George Mc-Clellan inching a 120,000-man army toward Richmond—any of these would have permitted Lincoln an easy excuse for ignoring a letter from a young bishop on a distant frontier. Besides, Whipple clumsily disclosed that he had failed to get Buchanan's attention: "I wrote to your predecessor and no notice was taken of it." But Whipple persisted. He was not asking much of Lincoln's time: "Will you not take a half hour to read my plea and so instruct the department that something like justice may be done a people whose cry calls for the vengeance of God?" The bishop included a 1,250-word précis of his idea for reforming Indian affairs, including a request that Lincoln select prominent, respected, and politically disinterested men to study the Indian office and recommend its thorough overhaul. What was needed, he said, was "a most careful examination of the whole subject by a committee of such pure men as I feel sure you will appoint." Whipple, characteristically, put forward no names— that should be left to Lincoln—just as he mentioned none of the corrupt officials he would like to see removed. Still, he made it clear just how unimpressed he was with the latter, the "John Does" rewarded purely for their "party work."[12]

Yet Lincoln did reply—briefly, but personally—less than a month later, enough to encourage the bishop that a professional relationship might be established between the two on this subject. Lincoln sent Whipple a note to say he had forwarded his letter and ideas to the Department of the Interior. In April, the bishop replied, in effect, twice. He first wrote, thanking Lincoln for passing on the original letter and recommendations to Secretary Smith. Then he followed up with a discussion of a singular problem that deeply marred white relations with Indians. Corrupt federal officials, determined to deprive Indians of their lands through unfair treaties, tended to cut deals with opportunists they cultivated among the tribes. The process bypassed the established chiefs and prominent men, damaging them politically and opening rifts within the tribes. "The government agents," Whipple wrote, "often depose the real chiefs and appoint or procure the appointment of others who are more pliable to carry out the plans of interested parties. The fear of this and his dependence on the government prevents decisions of character and in every way weakens the chief's influence with his people. He often becomes the creature of others powerful for mischief but powerless for good." That such a situation might create instability within the tribes and lead to a breakdown of peace on the frontier was clear.[13]

Lincoln's reply to Whipple's first letter also prompted Whipple to extend his lobbying. He wrote letters to Minnesota's congressional delegation. That produced mixed results. To Senator Morton Wilkinson, a Republican, he described the treatment of Native Americans as "shameless robbery." He warned Representative Cyrus Aldrich, also a Republican, that corrupt dealings with Indians amounted to "a grievous sin for which God will surely hold us accountable."[14] Neither man liked what he read and both told the bishop so. Whipple had better luck with the state's other senator, Democrat Henry Rice. A former fur trader with ties to the Ojibwes, Rice entered into a friendly correspondence with Whipple that extended well beyond the Dakota War and provided the bishop with a backdoor access to Lincoln in the autumn of 1862.

Whipple's decision in September 1862 to bring his campaign on behalf of the Indians to Washington coincided with a period of intense military anxiety in the nation's capital. His visit also roughly overlapped an acute period of theological reflection by Lincoln.

Earlier in the month, General Robert E. Lee had taken nearly forty thousand men on what would be his first invasion of the North, an effort to bring the war to the federal states and drive the recurring battles out of Virginia. His soldiers crossed the Potomac in western Maryland. Lincoln recalled General McClellan to command the main Northern army, and the general began a characteristically cautious pursuit.

Lincoln was also embarked on sorting out the greatest political challenge of his presidency. Since July, he had listened to and questioned those who would advise him on how to respond to slavery as a moral issue and an economic system that sustained the Southern economy and its war-making capacity. As the war persisted and intensified, Republicans, especially in the House of Representatives, argued the need to attack slavery directly. In the war's first year, Lincoln lacked a decisive policy for dealing with slaves who escaped to Union lines. He had reversed an order by General John Fremont freeing slaves in Missouri.

By the spring of 1862, it had become amply apparent that the war would run much longer and result in far greater bloodshed than anyone had imagined. On April 6 and 7—a week shy of the anniversary of Fort Sumter's surrender—more than a hundred thousand men clashed in the fields and woods around Shiloh Church, Tennessee, the largest battle in American history until then. In the chaotic contest, Major General Ulysses Grant narrowly achieved a victory over Confederates commanded by General Albert Sydney Johnston, who died in the first day's fighting. The battle produced an astonishing 23,700 casualties, a number greater than all the American lives lost in the Revolutionary War, the War of 1812, and the Mexican War combined.[15]

Ten days later, Lincoln signed a bill emancipating slaves in the District of Columbia. A less than radical measure, it compensated owners out of the U.S. Treasury at $300 for each person freed. But that marked a start in federal legislation against slavery. In June, the House passed a bill abolishing slavery in the

western territories. A month later, the president signed a "con-
fiscation bill," granting freedom to any slaves owned by soldiers
fighting for the Confederacy.[16]

By summer, such piecemeal measures trailed Lincoln's
thinking about the institution of slavery. He had come to regard
the problem in broader terms. How could he strike against the
system as a whole? Republican voices called for universal emancipation. Horace Greeley, editor of the *New-York Tribune*, challenged Lincoln on the issue, publishing on August 19 an open
letter, titled "The Prayer of Twenty Millions." Greeley charged
Lincoln with being "strangely and disastrously remiss in the dis-
charge of your official and imperative duty" in emancipating the
slaves.[17] As sternly worded as Greeley's piece was, it provided
Lincoln with the opportunity to disclose his thinking on the
issue publicly, by way of an essay, published in a Washington
newspaper on August 22. In a statement soon to become endur-
ingly famous, Lincoln said he would do whatever it took to save
the Union, whether that might include preserving slavery or extinguishing it.[18] That he so bluntly raised the possibility of the
latter excited those who would have him to do just that. But he
did not show his hand—and he offered little to impatient call-
ers, including those who claimed to speak on God's authority.

Lincoln's religious ideas are elusive. During his presidency,
he and his family attended New York Avenue Presbyterian
Church, but he left no clear evidence that would locate him
within any corner of conventional Christianity. Like many of
his time, he was thoroughly biblically literate (he also knew
Shakespeare well). By September 1862, the month Whipple
came to see him, Lincoln had begun a theological struggle over
the question of what a sovereign God might want of human affairs. God's will superseded frail human attempts to channel or
direct the divine power. In a private moment that month, Lincoln wrote a brief essay, giving full illustration to the perplexity
he felt. A document with powerful insight into human pride,

it is known as the "Meditation on the Divine Will," the name given it by John Hay, Lincoln's secretary, who discovered it in a desk drawer after the president's assassination.

"The will of God prevails," Lincoln wrote. "In great contests each party claims to act in accordance with the will of God. Both may be, and one must be, wrong. God cannot be for and against the same thing at the same time. In the present civil war it is quite possible that God's purpose is something different from the purpose of either party—and yet the human instrumentalities, working just as they do, are of the best adaptation to effect His purpose. I am almost ready to say that this is probably true—that God wills this contest, and wills that it shall not end yet. By his mere great power, on the minds of the now contestants, He could have either saved or destroyed the Union without a human contest. Yet the contest began. And, having begun He could give the final victory to either side any day. Yet the contest proceeds."[19]

By the time Lincoln met with Whipple, the president had also reached a decision about the fate of Lee's invasion. Were it to be beaten back, he would take that as a sign from God that it was time to end American slavery, in effect making its destruction the North's war aim, along with reuniting the nation. He would quietly share that decision with his cabinet the next Monday, September 21, after Lee's challenge had been defeated. Lincoln had the draft of the document in his desk when he agreed to receive Whipple.[20]

The bishop caught up with Lincoln shortly after the president had set a personal limit, too, on what he would allow in warfare. Lincoln stated plainly that he would temper justice with mercy. He made his policy clear in a letter sent a few weeks earlier to a Union supporter in Louisiana, whose Southern parishes had by then come under federal control. Interestingly, the letter is often quoted as evidence that the United States had entered a period of "total war," in which any illusions had been dispelled about Confederate states' willingness to return to the Union without a long and savage war. The first part of Lincoln's letter, replying to Colonel Cuthbert Bullitt, on July 28, 1862, appears to indicate that the president, exasperated with the war's progress, was calling for the Union to use all its resources to break Southern resistance. "What would you do in my position? Would you drop the war where it is? Or, would you prosecute it in future, with elder-stalk squirts, charged with rose water?" Lincoln rhetorically asked the loyalist Bullitt, recently appointed collector of customs in New Orleans. But then Lincoln shifted to a realism tempered by humility. "I am in no boastful mood. I shall not do more than I can, and I shall do all I can to save the government, which is my sworn duty as well as my personal inclination." That said, he made a crucial promise; he spoke here not only to Bullitt: "I shall do nothing in malice. What I deal with is too vast for malicious dealing."[21] The language foreshadowed the message Lincoln would deliver three years later, in his second inaugural address: "With malice toward none, with charity for all."

Was Whipple somewhat naïve in seeking out Lincoln at such a momentous time? Not if one looks at the late summer and early fall of 1862 as a truly revolutionary period in American history. That Lincoln had written some sort of emancipation document was widely rumored—and speculated upon in the press—in the month or so preceding September 22, when the president made it public. By its very nature, the document would distinguish Lincoln's presidency as a period of liberty's expansion comparable to the American Revolution and the Constitution that followed it. Whipple did not comment on the rumors about a proclamation, but he almost certainly would have read of them, enough to know he would be meeting with Lincoln at a time when what had seemed impossible less than a year earlier was now extremely close and certain. What better time, with a revolutionary act at hand, than to ask and argue for another change—not one so grand, but one that could curtail the duplicity and suffering to which another large segment of the population was subject? If justice were to be the order of the day for American slaves, then why not seek a form of it for Native Americans as well?

In 1862, the White House Whipple entered appeared, from the outside, much as it does now. A large portico sheltered visitors approaching the north side, facing Pennsylvania Avenue. Inside, however, the ambience was dark and heavy. Thick rugs covered the floors in the public rooms; large, gathered drapes shaded the windows, and big mahogany doors divided the various rooms.[22]

Whipple was taken upstairs to see Lincoln, in the president's office on the building's east side. On the walls hung maps detailing the main theaters of war, along with a portrait of former president Andrew Jackson, the great adversary of Native Americans. Lincoln kept his personal desk to one side of his office, near a central window with a view of the river. In the room's center sat a table used in cabinet meetings. He would have offered the bishop one of the several black walnut chairs kept in the room for officials and visitors alike.

Whipple, with his hand injured, took no notes of their climatic meeting, but he had a clear, long-rehearsed grasp of his main points. Here, face-to-face with Lincoln, he poured out his argument, detailing specific observations of the wrongs done the Indians and their dreadful results to individuals, families, and tribes. He described the poverty and degradation worked by unfair treaties. Whipple had come directly from an Indian war; he had seen the ultimate result of corruption and mistreatment. He knew that Lincoln, from his own experience with Black Hawk, had an idea of the dreadful damage such outbreaks could do. He also did not need to remind the president that, even as a distant conflict in a war whose military numbers paled in comparison with what the North and South threw at each other, there had been no such toll taken on civilians as on the prairies of Minnesota that summer.

Whipple sought a total reform of the Office of Indian Affairs. He knew what he wanted and he would have been succinct. He had seen up close the effects of alcohol sales, fraudulent dealing, and even violence by the men entrusted to keep the Indians' welfare in mind, rather than to enrich themselves.

At one point, Lincoln needed to pause and absorb the urgency of the message and register his own grasp of Whipple's information. It was characteristic of the president. He told Whipple a homespun story, providing an opportunity for them both to sit back a bit—and to show Whipple that he had heard him. "Bishop," he said, "a man thought that monkeys could pick cotton better than negroes could because they were quicker and their fingers smaller. He turned a lot of them into his cotton field, but he found that it took two overseers to watch one monkey. It needs more than one honest man to watch one Indian Agent."[23] The story pleased Whipple; he felt he had gotten through at last. Ten weeks later Lincoln would casually speak with a friend from Illinois whose brother-in-law Luther Dearborn had recently visited Minnesota. "When you see Lute," Lincoln told the friend, "ask him if he knows Bishop Whipple. He came here the other day and talked with me about the rascality of this Indian business until I felt it down to my boots."[24]

Lincoln made a promise after that meeting—poignantly, when viewed in retrospect—to address America's other racial sin after first dealing with slavery and secession. "If we get through this war," he said, "and I live, this Indian system shall be reformed!"[25]

How far Lincoln and Whipple discussed the Dakota War itself is impossible to know, but Whipple had no problem—as he made clear in many public statements—linking the mistreatment of Indians with the coming of violence. He drew a direct line between the two in Minnesota when he wrote about the war and its aftermath. He would not have left that connection unspoken. Yet he was not there to excuse individual or collective acts of violence by the Dakotas. The bishop believed in the necessity of justice. He had met white settlers wounded and traumatized by the fighting in Minnesota. He would later say that any Dakota found guilty of violence against civilians needed to be punished accordingly. He would steadfastly deny seeking clemency for any specific Dakota soldier arrested by Sibley. The logic of this is supported by the fact that the war had not ended by the time he saw Lincoln. It would be more than a week before Sibley began interning Dakotas he suspected of crimes, and more than two weeks before he set up a military court that would embark on a very rapid process of trying men accused of criminal activity in warfare. But in meeting with Lincoln when he did, Whipple got access to the president before Lincoln heard any extended discussion about the war from anyone else in Minnesota. What the bishop managed to do was set the war within the context of federal government corruption and ineptitude. He created for Lincoln a lens through which to view the war.

Whipple's visit also gained him more than the president's attention. Lincoln gave the bishop a vital asset to use in all his future arguments for reforming the Indian office. At the conclusion of their conversation, the president picked up one of his official cards and wrote on it a message to Caleb Smith, the interior secretary. Whipple, he said, was to have freedom of the department's archives,[26] meaning he could fully research federal treaties and official dealings with the Dakotas.

Whipple used his remaining time in Washington to investigate the records of the government's treaties with the Dakotas in 1851 and 1858.[27] It was while doing so that he learned about the battle fought between McClellan and Lee at Antietam Creek in western Maryland. Whipple secured a military pass to allow him to cross the Potomac on Union-controlled ferries and headed for the battlefield. He had heard that his friend, General Napoleon Dana, had been wounded in the fighting "and the Minnesota 1st badly cut up." He knew a number of the unit's men; he had preached to them at Fort Snelling in May 1861.[28]

At Antietam, the fighting had lasted from dawn to dusk on September 17, and the total number of men involved—112,000—exceeded that of even Shiloh. Lee fielded a smaller force than McClellan, but between the two armies, they left enough casualties to mark the engagement as the single bloodiest day in American history.

Whipple reached the battlefield on the 19th. The night before, Lee had withdrawn, leaving McClellan the tactical victor. Two days later, Union troops were still sorting the dead from the wounded. One sixteen-year-old Minnesotan, Charley Goddard, took time out to write to his mother: "If the horrors of war cannot be seen on this battlefield, they cant be seen any whare."[29] Whipple walked a ground splattered by the blood shed by opposing troops. For the second time in less than a month, he encountered people terribly wounded in battle—first in Saint Peter, where he served in the makeshift hospital, now in Maryland, where he returned to his role as spiritual comforter.

Writing to a friend, the bishop said the scene he witnessed "beggars description," but he tried anyway, lamenting "poor humanity, torn, mangled, tortured, dead, and to lie in a nameless grave." He also discerned elements of glory in the contest. "Much of it was a hand to hand and face to face conflict—bravely did our men stand up through that long day in the jaws of death." He spoke to the wounded and held a solemn service.[30]

Whipple spent the night in McClellan's tent, as his guest. Despite the stark changes in their circumstances, the general still recognized a friendship that had begun when Whipple served as a priest in Chicago and McClellan was a railroad man. The two talked for three hours, then prayed together before going to sleep. A few days later, Whipple wrote to McClellan, describing his visits to the military hospitals on the battlefield. "I had the opportunity to commend some dying men to God and to whisper the Saviour's name in their ear for the last journey."[31]

Eight

Maintaining the Pressure

AFTER VISITING THE BATTLEFIELD AT ANTIETAM, Bishop Whipple traveled nearly two months in the Northeast. To be distant from Minnesota during this period, with the Dakota War still simmering and Dakota prisoners awaiting trial, seems an odd choice, but Whipple perceived that he had a singular opportunity to press the reform of the federal Indian system and to do it on a public stage. He would also be able to directly tap old friends in the business world for donations to help Minnesota's refugees.

The Protestant Episcopal Church planned to convene its General Convention, its governing body, in New York City on October 1. The church met every three years, moving the meeting's location as befitted the church's status as a national organization. At the previous meeting, in Richmond in October 1859, Whipple's fellow bishops had consecrated him to their ranks. This year, he joined his fellow Northern prelates—twenty-two in all—on the event's opening day. Some who attended the convention, which met in Saint John's Chapel in an upper-class Manhattan neighborhood, came prepared to seek a church statement criticizing rebellious Southern members. (Southern Episcopalians held their own convention that year.)

But outspokenness ran counter to the church's tradition of keeping silent on social and political issues. On October 9, the *New York Times* ran an editorial voicing hope that the tradition of not speaking on secular affairs would be broken this time around and the church would make some declaration against secession. But the paper also noted, "It is but seldom that the Episcopal Church has felt called upon to take any notice of national affairs, and that conservative and exclusive habit which ordinarily restricts its councils to the consideration of matters purely ecclesiastical, will undoubtedly incline many of its members to silence even at so critical a moment in our country's history."[1] It may seem strange that the church as a body had not officially spoken out about slavery and disunion. That tradition of public reserve made a decision by Whipple all the more remarkable—especially for its success.

Whipple arrived at the convention still the church's newest bishop. Perhaps because of his relative isolation on the frontier, or the urgency he felt about reforming the Indian system, he immediately challenged the bishops to speak out on the latter. At the time the convention opened, Whipple hardly seemed prepared for a fight. He had, after all, visited the wounded from two battlefields in a single month. He felt uncharacteristically lethargic and even depressed. In addition, he still felt pain in his hand from the injury he had sustained during his ministrations in Saint Peter. Nevertheless, he would not let his new acquaintance with Lincoln rest; he was determined to push his cause with both the president and the eastern public, a decision made more urgent by the crucial moment at which white–Indian relations stood in his state.

Whipple summoned strength to write a three-page statement about Indian affairs. He wanted his fellow bishops not only to endorse it but also sign their names to it, thereby making it a national petition. He proposed to get it to the White House by the convention's end on October 17. But before he could bring the document to the floor, another bishop—to whom Whipple showed a draft—cut him off, with icy condescension. "I hope you are not going to bring politics into the House," the cleric said. The remark enraged Whipple. His anger became obvious enough to bring Bishop Alonzo Potter of Pennsylvania rushing to his side. "My diocese," Whipple said, as through gritted teeth, "is desolated by Indian war; eight hundred of our people are dead, and I have just come from a hospital for the wounded and dying. I asked one of my brothers to sign this paper and he responds by calling it 'politics.'"[2] Whipple, who knew politics from his own younger experience, regarded his statement as one built on moral grounds, not mere partisan appeal.

It proved fortunate that Potter got to him first. The bishop had a geographical background in common with Whipple, and he understood, too, how a clergyman could speak passionately about worldly issues he regarded as morally transcendent. Although a longtime resident of Pennsylvania, Potter had close ties to upstate New York. He had served in the region as a professor and a college president. He also felt strongly antagonistic toward slavery, about which he had written, and he well understood the basic indignation Whipple felt, along with the imperative to speak from it. Crucially, Potter decided on the spot to take charge of Whipple's statement and shepherd it through the convention. "My dear Minnesota," he said, "give the paper to me." He promised to get it signed. Furthermore, Potter said that he and Bishop Charles McIlvaine of Ohio would take it directly to Lincoln after the convention.[3]

Whipple would have appreciated the significance of both Potter's promises. McIlvaine, a Princeton graduate, held a status in the church as a leading intellectual and in the federal government as an astute diplomat. The previous year, Lincoln had sent him to Great Britain to argue the case among his fellow Anglicans that the British government should not recognize the Confederate states as a sovereign nation. Later that October, when McIlvaine visited Washington, Secretary of State William Seward referred him to Lincoln, describing the Ohio bishop as "our excellent friend."[4] (Later still, Whipple would make sure Lincoln received a second copy of the same document; he left nothing to chance.)

To what did the bishops put their names? The document is clearly Whipple's, with a tone respectful and also pointed. At about six hundred words, the statement could be summarized in a short sentence: abuse of Indians produces war, so it is in everyone's interest that Indians not be abused. Like the classic formula for a standard American sermon, the statement makes its point three times over. It declares that point near the beginning, elaborates on it later, and then repeats it near the conclusion. Treat the Indians as wards of the state, the document said, protect them from theft and violence, and make sure their annuities are paid toward purposes that allow them to sustain themselves. As Whipple himself had recommended to Lincoln in his letter in March, the bishops called for creation of "a Commission of men of high character, who have no political ends to subserve, to whom may be referred this whole question, in order that they may devise a more perfect system for the administration of Indian affairs."[5]

Lincoln would have recognized the argument, having just heard it from Whipple in person, but the bishops' statement carried an impact well beyond what even a relentless forty-year-old prelate could pull off alone. As the *New York Times* had noted, the bishops were not given to speaking out on public affairs. Yet this time, eighteen of them did so. And they had the public backing of twenty others who had signed the statement, from prominent rectors to laymen, including an assistant justice of the Minnesota Supreme Court. Signatories ranged geographically from the border states that had proved so crucial to the Union's early survival—Missouri, Kentucky, Maryland, and Delaware—to their Northern neighbors. Upon receiving the statement, Lincoln held in his hands as close to a declaration of consensus as he was ever likely to receive from the leaders of the Episcopal Church, whose communicants included many powerful and prominent men and women in the United States. Whipple had gone far beyond anything he had previously attempted in his efforts at reforming the Indian office. He had crafted a national petition that was placed directly before the president.

Whipple did not stop there. On Sunday, October 5, he took his message public, preaching in a Broadway church on the need for a complete overhaul of the way the government treated the Indians. A reporter for the *New York Times* covered the sermon at length. The next day's story carried some familiar Whipple statements ("The American Indian is more brave, more truthful and more virtuous than any other heathen on earth"), but Whipple also disclosed some of the fruits of his time spent in studying the Department of the Interior archives in Washington the previous month. He accused the government of falsely dealing with the Ojibwes and Dakotas, taking their lands in exchange for empty promises of just reimbursement, this without full agreement from the tribes. The bishop, the *New York Times* reporter said, charged the government with "the nonpayment of $100,000 due to the Lower Sioux; payments now withheld and demanded in vain, and the actual starving to death of the children of chiefs for absolute want, owing to this neglect; women destroyed by brutal violence, and cruel robberies committed by the whites." It was strong stuff, and Whipple did not hesitate to say it had terrible consequences. What he described, the bishop said, "had been the dreadful causes that had led to the recent outbreaks and massacres, unparalleled in Indian annals, and against these causes he, and all who were in the service of Christ, had plead, and protested, and written to Washington in vain."[6]

Such a sermon was calculated to produce an impression on those who heard it in New York, center of the nation's com-

munications and economic power. Whipple meant it to be discussed, talked over, and shared. His timing was particularly
important. His persistence—first in Washington, then among
his fellow bishops in New York—provided a counterweight, for
the president and the eastern public, to the hatred of Indians
that continued to build up in Minnesota.

On September 28, three days before the Episcopal Church's
convention opened, Colonel Sibley ordered a five-member
military tribunal to "try *summarily* the mulatto, mixed bloods,
and Indians engaged in the Sioux raids and massacres."[7] The
commission included two colonels, two captains, and a first
lieutenant. (One of the original appointees would shortly step
down; Sibley would replace him with a major.) Sibley also
chose a Saint Paul lawyer, Isaac Heard, to act as the trials' re-
corder and take notes. Heard had been serving on Sibley's staff.
(From his unique vantage point, he would gather the resources
to write a commercial book about the war, published in 1864.)
But before any of the Dakotas could be brought before the
military commission, they would have to be charged with one
or more crimes.

In this instance, Rev. Stephen Riggs, the Presbyterian missionary and longtime resident among the tribe, played an important role. He spoke Dakota and personally knew many
Indians who had been detained by Sibley's forces. After Sibley's
victory in the Battle of Wood Lake ended the war, a substantial
peace party of Dakotas who had never supported Little Crow
negotiated the safe transfer of 263 men, women, and children
taken captive during the war. The majority were of mixed white
and Indian background. All were turned over to Sibley at Camp
Release, forty miles northwest of Little Crow's village. The site
lay close to Lac Qui Parle, where Riggs had worked many years.[8]

Hundreds of Dakota men entered Sibley's camp—either
having surrendered or been captured—after the hostilities

ended. Riggs might have questioned them closely one by one—a time-consuming, if careful, measure—but instead he relied on the individual Dakotas he trusted to provide him truthful information to ferret out the men who had allegedly committed especially heinous acts during the war. Isaac Heard, who was on the scene, later told how Riggs got his information. "He obtained it," Heard wrote, "by assembling the half-breeds, and others possessed of means of knowledge, in a tent, and interrogating them concerning suspected parties. The names of witnesses were appended to the charge." The missionary, Heard said, "was, in effect, the grand jury of the court."[9] Riggs's method allowed him to work with great speed. Within three days, the information he had gathered permitted Sibley to bring charges against nearly four hundred Indians.

On October 9, General Pope telegraphed General Halleck in Washington with welcome, if belated, news: "The Sioux war may be considered at an end." Pope estimated that fifteen hundred Dakotas had come into Sibley's camp. He mentioned the trials and made it clear that he expected the ultimate penalty awaited the accused. "Many are being tried by military commission for being connected in the late horrible outrages, and will be executed." In the meantime, he said, "I have disarmed all, and will bring them down to Fort Snelling until the Government shall decide what to do with them."[10]

Observers then and later noted several remarkable aspects of the trials. The five-man panel acted with great speed, at times disposing of dozens of cases in a day. After the first trial, the panel made an extraordinary use of the man it had just convicted, effectively turning him into an inquisitor of subsequent prisoners. He performed the task with gusto. That man was known, interchangeably, by his Dakota and English names: Otakle and Godfrey, respectively. Born to African American and Dakota parents, he faced charges of having murdered seven men, women, and children near New Ulm, as well as participating in other violent actions. Four people prepared to testify against him. Yet despite the gravity of the charges he faced, Godfrey made a surprisingly positive impression on his judges. "He had such an honest look, and spoke with such a truthful tone, that the court, though prejudiced against him in the beginning, were now unanimously inclined to believe that there were possibilities as to his sincerity."[11]

Godfrey spoke English haltingly, a trait that, together with his soft voice, apparently worked to his favor, Heard reported. It helped, too, that no single witness testified that he or she actually saw him kill anyone—although three former captives said he had boasted of murdering civilians. The tribunal took its time with Godfrey, eventually clearing him of the charge of murder at New Ulm while finding him guilty of participating in other killings. They gave him a death sentence but recommended it be commuted to ten years' imprisonment.[12]

Godfrey's story might have ended there, as far as the commission was concerned, but it did not—a memorable feature of an unorthodox judicial proceeding. The officers kept Godfrey in the room and, as they went through the cases, asked him to question the accused as they were brought forward. He rose to the occasion, laughing with open skepticism at many Dakotas who protested their innocence. He spoke out, contradicting their statements. Godfrey impressed Heard, who presented his recollection of the testimony without irony: "He was the means of bringing to justice a large number of the savages, in every instance but two his testimony being substantiated by the subsequent admission of the Indians themselves. His observation and memory were remarkable. Not the least thing had escaped his eye or ear."[13] Godfrey remembered the types of guns each Dakota soldier carried, along with their lances and knives, where they stood at a particular event, and how they carried out a killing. "It was a study to watch him, as he sat in court, scanning the face of every culprit who came in with the eye of a cat about to spring."[14] On their first day, the panel had found themselves a nearly omniscient witness to the war.

As the trials progressed, the panel moved quickly. Some trials had lasted only a few minutes. The language of the court was English, which was unfamiliar to many of the accused. On October 21, Sibley telegraphed General Pope in Saint Paul: "More than 120 cases have been disposed of, the greater part of whom have been found guilty of murder and other atrocious crimes." Nearly 300 still awaited trial.[15] Within two weeks, those proceedings were complete, and by November 3, the remaining trials had taken place, 42 on that final day.[16] The tribunal sentenced 303 Dakotas to the gallows and another 18 to terms in jail. Executing so many would be a massive task, requiring careful planning and logistics. Would the condemned be hanged sequentially in groups, or at once, from a massive platform? Isaac Heard, with a touch of defensiveness, focused on what he considered the logic and necessity of the verdicts. Without identifying anyone, he wrote, "Some people have thought that the haste with which the accused were tried must have prevented any accuracy as to the ascertainment of their complicity." But that would be a misjudgment, he said, as all that was needed for conviction was an Indian to affirm he had been in the battle at New Ulm or Fort Ridgely, and had fired on whites. "The officers composing the court were well known to the community as respectable and humane gentlemen."[17]

Once the trials ended, Lincoln became the focus of a high-profile lobbying campaign to carry out the death sentences, in full. Pope sent him a telegram, containing the names of all 303 of the condemned. It cost the government $400, irritating Lincoln, who advised the general that further communication on the subject should be by mail. Governor Ramsey shortly followed with his own telegram to the president: "I hope the execution of every Sioux Indian condemned by the military court will be at once ordered. It would be wrong upon principle and policy to refuse this." The governor went a good deal further, raising the possibility that if the president did not accept the court's verdict, Minnesotans' outrage might threaten civil order. The state's population could become a lynch mob.

Ramsey may have been the first to suggest the possibility to Lincoln; he was not the last. The specter of a total failure of law and order—of a counter-massacre against the Dakotas—became a theme in messages sent to Lincoln, urging him to sign off on the mass hanging. "Private revenge," Ramsey said, "would . . . take the place of official judgment on these Indians."[18] Ramsey may have reached that conclusion based on actual events that fall. In October, army soldiers moved a caravan of Dakota women, children, and older men from Sibley's camp to Fort Snelling. The group came under attack outside New Ulm, as a mob of angry whites armed with stones assaulted the wagons. Soldiers pushed them back, but not before they had injured several people.[19]

On November 10, Lincoln indicated that he wanted to study the verdicts; there would be nothing automatic about his response to the military court. He asked General Pope for details of the trials. "Please forward as soon as possible the full and complete record of their convictions; and if the record does not fully indicate the more guilty and influential of the culprits, please have a careful statement made on these points and forwarded to me."[20] Pope replied the next day, promising to send the records on, but he could not help himself responding to Lincoln's assumption that some of the condemned might be "more guilty and influential" than others. The president should not assume such a distinction, said the general. "I desire to represent to you that the only distinction between the culprits is as to which of them murdered most people or violated most young girls. All of them are guilty of these things in more or less degree."[21]

Like Ramsey, Pope wanted Lincoln to know the mood in

Minnesota, but the general allowed himself more liberty in describing it. "The people of this State, most of whom had relations or connections thus barbarously murdered and brutally outraged are exasperated to the last degree, and if the guilty are not all executed I think it nearly impossible to prevent the indiscriminate massacre of all the Indians old men, women, and children. The soldiers guarding them are from this State and equally connected and equally incensed with the citizens."[22] So, it was not just civil order but military discipline that was fragile. Lincoln held the state's peace in his hands. Indeed, Pope made that warning twice, returning at the end of his telegram to tell Lincoln that young women who had been held captive were now "distributed about among the towns bearing the marks of the terrible outrages committed upon them, while daily there are funerals of those massacred men, women, and children whose bodies are being daily found. These things influence the public mind to a fearful degree, and your action has been awaited with repressed impatience."[23] Pope also wanted Lincoln to know that the Dakotas should be considered as traitors—surely candidates for the death penalty—as well as felons. They were not "wild Indians," the general said, but had for years lived on government largesse—the annuity payments. Furthermore, Pope said, these killers knew their victims, "people among whom they had lived for years in constant and intimate intercourse, at whose houses they had slept, and at whose tables they had been fed." In the general's view, the Dakotas had taken the government's money and then turned on and murdered their neighbors.[24]

Word of the call for raw revenge began to reach Whipple on his travels. Whipple, who wrote sparingly in September and October because of the lingering injury to his hand, did not comment on the war's end or the formation of a military commission to try Dakota soldiers. Instead, he had focused his attention on his church's convention. But he had other duties to which he had to attend. Benjamin Wright, his father-in-law, died while on a business trip, requiring the bishop to supervise the return of his body and its interment in Adams, New York. He also received requests that he serve as guest preacher in churches as far away as Boston. While in New York during the church convention, he also began a new project, raising money to help Minnesotans displaced by the war.[25]

By late October, though, his hand had begun to heal and he resumed his correspondence. In a letter to his daughter Elizabeth on October 24, he apologized for his silence and also described how he had tried over the past week to solicit contributions from New York businessmen to help the refugees in Minnesota. The problem was, he said, getting "the ear of this great busy babbling New York." But, in fact, he had done so. Ever since his first posting as a priest in Rome, New York, Whipple had shown himself a skilled fund-raiser. He told "darling Lizzie" that he had organized a three-man committee and, the day before, raised $1,500, which he entrusted to his close friend, a wealthy businessman named Robert Minturn. Minturn ran a shipping company and was an owner of a famous clipper ship, the *Flying Cloud*, which had taken men to the California goldfields a decade earlier. "I hope to be able to alleviate suffering," the bishop wrote his daughter, referring to the money he had raised. "It is always glad work."[26]

Within a fortnight, Whipple also reached out to Governor Ramsey, then in the midst of lobbying Lincoln for a mass hanging. The bishop wrote the governor to tell him he could expect a check for $2,500 from Minturn (a sum roughly equivalent to $70,000 today). The bishop said he believed more money would be forthcoming. "I may get a few hundred dollars here altho[ugh] my time here will be devoted to my own church work," he said. Notably, Whipple did nothing to hide his opinions about the Dakota War from Ramsey, who drew from the conflict radically different lessons. "I feel a deep solicitude for our poor sufferers," Whipple wrote, "More because this outbreak is wholly owing to a bad system of Indian affairs." He blamed the system for leaving Indians without legal protection and open to the worst influences of whites. And, the bishop continued, "at last we wonder [that] we have reaped what we sowed."[27]

Whatever satisfaction Ramsey took in Whipple's fund-raising, he did not reciprocate the bishop's view of the war. He remained adamantly supportive of the military commission's sentences. So did others, some quite politically influential. In Saint Paul, residents petitioned for the hanging; Senator Wilkinson, with two Minnesota Congressmen, urged Lincoln, "let the Law be executed."[28] Pope suggested Lincoln could relieve himself of the responsibility, if he preferred. Pope recommended the president simply turn the convicted Dakotas over to Minnesota authorities. Pope apparently had begun to worry that Lincoln, taking his time, did not fully grasp the brutality of the war or the fury of the North Star State's white citizens. Telegraphing Lincoln, he said, "I would suggest that if the Gov't be unwilling at so great distance to order the execution of the condemned Indians the Criminals be turned over to the State Gov't to be dealt with."[29]

By mid-November, Whipple prepared to return to Minnesota. He got back in time to learn fully about the trials, and also about how Stephen Riggs had begun to doubt their complete justice. Riggs's concern arose after he received a letter from Jane Williamson, who lived near the reservation. She had scanned the list of the men sentenced to die and become alarmed when she saw it included the name of a Dakota man she credited with rescuing her during the worst of the fighting. On Friday, November 14, she sat down at her desk and wrote to Riggs. She described to him how she and others had been saved near the Upper Sioux Agency by an Indian named Tapaytatanka and his friends. He had told them about the impending hostilities and then protected them. Yet the military court had convicted him and sentenced him to death. In her letter, Williamson went beyond merely raising the alarm that an innocent man might face the gallows. She showed, too, that she had given a great deal of thought to the moral situation in which individuals might find themselves in wartime. To Riggs, she raised a subtle and nuanced question about how good-willed but less-than-daring people survived when the world seemed to collapse around them. The Dakotas who wanted nothing to do with the war may have been inhibited from acting beneficently to white neighbors through the mortal fear that they themselves would be killed, either by the warriors among them or by whites mistaking them for enemies, she said. "I suppose none of us can fully realize the circumstances in which our friendly Indians were thus placed[. N]ot wishing to participate in the deeds of Little Crow, many would gladly have fled to our Flag and espoused our cause, but how should they get away and how would they be received?"[30]

Williamson's letter gave Riggs pause—but not for long. On Monday, November 17, he wrote directly to Lincoln, identifying himself as a missionary with long experience of the Dakotas and also as the man who had served as chaplain in Sibley's command. Riggs displayed a bit of ambivalence over the death sentences; he seemed to struggle, in his letter, to convince himself that the right course was being followed. To execute so many would be "terrible," he said, yet it also seemed unavoidable. "My long acquaintance with these Indians and personal acquaintance with many of those who are condemned would naturally lead me to desire that no greater punishment be inflicted upon them than is required by justice." That sounded as if Riggs might be questioning the wisdom of the military commission. He also took public opinion seriously. "But knowing the excited state of this part of the country—the indignation which is felt against the whole Indian people in consequence of these murders and outrages—this indignation being often unreasonable and wicked, venting itself on the innocent as well as the guilty—knowing this I feel that a great necessity is upon us to execute the great majority of those who have been condemned by the Military Commission."[31] Riggs portrayed himself as a man caught in a moral dilemma, regarding the justice rendered by the military court as imperfect but also believing the executions might head off a lawless desire among Minnesotans for revenge.

In writing to Lincoln, Riggs chose a course that Whipple had not: he named names. The missionary directly asked Lincoln to consider commuting the death sentences of five men out of the 303 condemned. Bearing in mind Jane Williamson's testimony, he asked for mercy for Tapaytatanka and for two other Indians he identified only by the numbers on the list of men the military had compiled as condemned. None had participated in the killing, he assured the president.[32]

Riggs's letter closely followed one other, this from an official within Lincoln's government who questioned the moral wisdom of allowing such a mass execution. In Washington, William Dole, commissioner of Indian affairs, called the plans to hang the 303 out of keeping with American religious ideals. He expressed his doubts that the judgment ought to be completely upheld. On November 10, as Ramsey and Pope clamored for Lincoln's approval for the mass execution, Dole wrote a three-page letter to his superior, Caleb Smith, secretary of the interior, and asked Smith to pass it to Lincoln. Dole said he sympathized with the people of Minnesota and did not doubt the legality and integrity of the military commission. But, he said, "it seems to me that an indiscriminate punishment of men who have laid down their arms and surrendered themselves as prisoners, partakes more of the character of revenge than the infliction of deserved punishment; that is contrary to the spirit of the age, and our character as a great, magnanimous, and Christian people." Smith read the letter and sent it to Lincoln the next day.[33]

On the trains back to Minnesota, Bishop Whipple took time to study more closely the notes he had taken in the Office of Indian Affairs regarding the government's treaties that had deprived the Dakotas of their lands in 1851 and 1858. He began to amplify what he had briefly mentioned in his October 5 sermon in New York. His fear of government dishonesty had been "all confirmed" by his research, he wrote to Rev. Ezekiel Gear, a priest in northern Minnesota with whom he often exchanged letters. Whipple singled out the journey that the Dakota chiefs had made to Washington in 1858, during which they had signed a treaty parting with half their reservation, nearly one million acres on the north side of the Minnesota River. The Mdewakanton and the smaller Wahpekute bands were to receive $96,000, the bishop said. "Although four years have elapsed since that sale, these Indians have never received a cent of that money. $800.58 is to their credit on the books of the Dept. and all else has gone for claims." Four years after the agreement, the Dakotas experienced a long delay, waiting for their annuity in the summer of 1862—"at last the outbreak came and it desolated 200 miles of our border."[34]

Whipple, amidst his anger over uncovering such direct evidence of fraud, came very close to making an uncharacteristic mistake and alienating his closest friend in Congress, a man with whom he had always had a pleasant correspondence. Senator Henry Rice, the Democrat whose term as one of Minnesota's first two senators would end the next year, had treated Whipple respectfully and attentively from their first correspondence, even though they had never personally met. The bishop said as much in a brief letter he wrote to him from Carlisle, Pennsylvania, on November 12, as he entrained to Minnesota. "You are the only public man who from the first has recognized the justice of my plea." Whipple discussed his goal of building up sentiment for a reform of the Indian system among a broad public. He also enclosed another copy of the bishops' statement. He asked

Rice to lay it before Lincoln, as had Bishop Potter the previous month. But then Whipple lashed out at the injustice of the 300 death sentences. By then, Whipple had come to the conclusion that the sentences appeared much like an order to massacre captive soldiers to make sure a handful of war criminals did not escape. Perhaps Whipple did not realize how his words might sound to Rice, a man hearing a very different argument from other constituents impatient that the hangings proceed. "[W]e cannot hang men by the hundreds," the bishop declared. "Upon our own premises we have no right to do so. We claim that they are an independent nation and as such they are prisoners of war. The leaders must be punished but we cannot afford by any wanton cruelty to purchase a long Indian war—nor by injustice in other matters purchase the anger of God."[35]

It may have been the phrase "wanton cruelty" that inflamed Rice. He wrote Whipple back a letter that showed him in the grip of such outrage that he found himself unable to finish it in a single sitting. "I think you are in error in saying that they are prisoners of war—in my opinion they are murderers of the deepest dye," Rice wrote. "The laws of war cannot be so far distorted as to reach this case in any respect, when I reflect that without a moment's notice they struck upon unoffending men, women, and children from many of whom they had received many kindnesses—and butchered them ere they had time to commend their souls to God—When I know that they opened the throbbing womb of the mother and tore therefrom the unborn infant and dashed out its brains against the dead mother's head—When I know that the squaws held the young helpless white girl until savages gratified their beastly passions until life relieved the victim—When I know that infants were nailed to trees alive and there left to die in sight of their captive mothers—would I spare them? No, never! Every guilty one should perish—not one should be spared that he might hereafter boast to the Indians of the plains of his brutal feats." Rice had heard the atrocity stories and he did not doubt them. After venting his anger, he got up from his writing table to compose himself. He returned to finish the letter, writing in slightly lighter ink. What is remarkable is that the senator did not give up on the bishop. Instead, he explained his reaction. "When I sat down to write, I only intended to acknowledge the receipt of your note, and to give you assurance of my cordial cooperation but as my mind became fixed upon the subject my hand penned the running thoughts."[36] Rice's letter showed how deeply the alienation of Minnesota's whites from the state's Indians had penetrated. The senator took the atrocity stories seriously, even if he did not publicly clamor for the Dakotas' execution, as Pope and Ramsey were doing. Still, his opinion showed how lonely Whipple's position was.

Whipple was fortunate that when Senator Rice promised his cooperation, he meant it. Rice saw Lincoln the next day and gave him the copy of the bishops' statement, along with a cover letter in which Rice said he concurred with it. "For the honor of the government, the welfare of our frontier citizens, and that of the Indians, I most earnestly join the prayers made to Your Excellency by so many distinguished and good men."[37]

Nine

Judgment and Reason

TWO WEEKS AFTER BISHOP WHIPPLE RETURNED HOME to Faribault, Abraham Lincoln delivered his second annual message to Congress, a detailed account of the executive branch's activities during the previous year. The president wrote the message—a predecessor to the State of the Union address—to be read, rather than delivered as a speech. In the December 1 document, he included sections on foreign affairs, the federal budget, the sale of public lands, and much else. Lincoln dealt at length with the most momentous decision of his two-year-old presidency: his order emancipating all slaves held within rebel territory. It would take effect by month's end, unless the eleven secessionist states ended their rebellion and returned to the Union. None showed any signs of doing so. By January 1, 1863, then, the Emancipation Proclamation became law, a great step toward freeing nearly four million men, women, and children and extinguishing American slavery forever. Lincoln wrote for the occasion. Departing from the dry tone that marked much of the document, he chose language worthy of the moment. "In giving freedom to the slave we assure freedom to the free—honorable alike in what we give and what we preserve."[1]

Whipple, studying the message reprinted in the newspapers, found with pleasure that it contained more—a brief but unmistakable reference to the object of all his lobbying. One-third the way through the document, Lincoln mentioned that Congress might consider taking up reform of government deal-ings with Native Americans, the culturally diverse group with whom blacks and whites shared the United States. Lincoln said he had received persuasive advice that the relationship with the Indians could be much improved, to the benefit of all.

Lincoln's remarks on the Indians were brief, taking up only two paragraphs in a long document. The first paragraph re-ferred to a visit to Washington by a Cherokee chief. The second was more compelling in its narrative. Lincoln introduced the topic by describing his horror at another war, one fought largely against white civilians. "In the month of August last the Sioux Indians in Minnesota attacked the settlements in their vicinity with extreme ferocity, killing indiscriminately men, women, and children. This attack was wholly unexpected." Lincoln said those who perished were largely undefended, and that possibly as many as eight hundred people died. Much property had been destroyed. "The State of Minnesota has suffered great injury from this Indian war," Lincoln wrote. "A large portion of her territory has been depopulated, and a severe loss has been sus-tained by the destruction of property. The people of that State manifest much anxiety for the removal of the tribes beyond the limits of the State as a guaranty against future hostilities. The Commissioner of Indian Affairs will furnish full details."[2]

On this rather ominous note, Lincoln might have ended his report. (Much more would shortly be heard from Minnesotans calling for exiling the state's Indians.) But the president then added a coda notably different in tone. He alluded to the pos-sibility that such violence as had happened there might be pre-vented in the future. "I submit for your especial consideration whether our Indian system shall not be remodeled. Many wise and good men have impressed me with the belief that this can be profitably done." He named no names—it would hardly be fitting to do so in such a formal document—but the sentences indicated that Bishop Whipple, through his letters, his White House visit, and his petitions, had gotten through to Lincoln. He had placed a rational proposal on the table before the president and the president in turn was passing it on to the nation.

Whipple wasted no time in sending Lincoln his thanks, in a short letter in which he repeated his central point—as if Lincoln by then did not thoroughly recognize it—that government dealings with the Indians had long constituted "a stupendous piece of wickedness."[3]

Lincoln had yet to decide whether to allow his army to carry out the death sentences of 303 Dakotas in Minnesota. On the day Lincoln delivered his annual message to Congress, he also asked Joseph Holt, his judge advocate, whether the decision could be delegated to others—as General Pope had argued—or whether it lay entirely with him. Holt advised Lincoln that only he could make the decision. Lincoln's question had been pro forma, but the response clarified the situation for all.[4]

While Minnesota awaited that news, Whipple launched a new public project, as ambitious as his lobbying of Lincoln but for a markedly different audience. This time, he would address his fellow Minnesotans and his goal was simple, if audacious: to persuade them to temper their demands for revenge with mercy. The document would be his most important essay on the Dakota War. He focused on the moral questions confronting white Minnesotans as the war's victors. At the very time when many were demanding a mass hanging and warning lynch mobs would take the matter into their own hands if such an execution did not occur, Whipple appealed to Minnesotans to examine their consciences. Think reasonably, put aside your rage, he counseled. In so writing, he made a bold and risky move. Identified by some as overly sympathetic to the Indians, Whipple had already been threatened with mob violence himself.

At this point, many men in Whipple's shoes—motivated by religious principles or not—might well have backed off, sensing the danger to their reputations and possibly their bodies. But Whipple saw his essay into print, and he sent Lincoln a copy. On December 3, with the president's decision still hanging in the balance, the *Saint Paul Pioneer* and other newspapers published "The Duty of Citizens Concerning the Indian Massacre." In it, Whipple provided a summary of his ideas and described his research in Washington into the Dakota treaties. He also rebuked talk of vigilantism or mob violence as both inherently undemocratic and unchristian. "Punishment loses its lesson when it is the vengeance of a mob," he wrote. "The mistaken cry, 'Take law into our own hands!' is the essence of rebellion." That sentence carried considerable resonance, secular and theological. As everyone in Minnesota understood, rebellion was the secessionists' crime. It threatened the existence of a nation many regarded as having a special place in God's favor. In addition, the South's rebellion had already consumed thousands of lives. Minnesotans had contributed generously to defending the nation's integrity.[5]

Theologically, too, rebellion was Satan's sin. In the thinking of many Christians, the devil and his angels had dared to challenge God. They had undertaken an evil course. (Whipple returned to this issue again shortly. A condemnation of rebellion undergirded the sermon he preached at month's end—in the city of Mankato, where the Dakota prisoners were then held and where they were to be executed.)

In "The Duty of Citizens," a reader may discern Whipple at his most elemental, following his mother's Christian commandment to him as a child to place himself on the side of the weak and oppressed, because that would be where God always was to be found. But the essay also represented a political act. In writing it, the bishop worked to apply an insight he was gaining through his lobbying of Washington. If he wanted reform, he had to alter public opinion and get people on his side. To do otherwise, he risked being a lone voice, righteous but isolated. His training and experience as a clergyman helped with the task. His work as a priest lay in persuading people to recognize and act on truth. He never described himself as an "enthusiast"—a label given revivalists who played on the emotions to win converts—so his ally was in speaking plainly and reasonably. Time and again, whether writing to presidents or making his case in public essays, he followed a linear course: logic dictates fair treatment of the Indians because it will produce a social peace underlain by justice. Furthermore, a nation that called itself Christian required its citizens to act humanely, especially toward those most vulnerable.

By the time he wrote his essay, Whipple had reached a full understanding of the Dakota War, including its effect on the public imagination in Minnesota. But his appeal would, by its nature, challenge the grief and loss expressed by the refugees and, even more so, spur the rage of extremists whose views found an audience in the wake of the war's trauma. Some of those people had easy access to print media, enough to raise their public profiles to influence within the state. They knew what they wanted and their views were not something the bishop shared. For example, Jane Grey Swisshelm, an editor with strong connections to the state's Republican Party, ran a newspaper called the *Saint Cloud Democrat*, in which she denounced slavery, supported women's rights, and—until the war—pondered whether Indians might be integrated into white society. A Pennsylvanian, she had moved to the North Star State with her young daughter, Zo, in 1857. During the Dakota War, she turned rabidly against the Indians, whose extermination she frankly demanded. She heavily garnished her inflammatory editorials with capital letters and exclamation points. If 303 Dakotas did not swing from federally sponsored gallows, then the survivors ought to be lynched. "Get ready," she wrote, "and as soon as these convicted murderers are turned loose, shoot them and be sure they are shot dead, dead, DEAD, DEAD!"[6]

Whipple and Swisshelm may have encountered each other before the war. The editor visited Faribault in 1860 and stayed long enough to become acquainted with an Ojibwe girl being educated in the Episcopal Church school there. Swisshelm liked what she saw and wrote that "under proper training" Native Americans might reach white standards of civilization. Like Whipple, she declared herself dead set against liquor dealing and in favor of teaching the Indians agriculture.[7] The war never touched her home city of Saint Cloud. But Little Crow's raids into nearby counties brought it close enough to have enraged her. She called on the state legislature to offer a ten-dollar bounty on every Dakota scalp taken. More potently, she declared, "A Sioux has just as much right to life as a hyena, and he who would spare them is an enemy to his race."[8] Before year's end, Swisshelm handed control of her newspaper to a relative and hit the lecture circuit in the East. She made a specialty of describing atrocities. In 1863, she went to Washington to try to lobby Lincoln against showing any generosity toward Native Americans.

In Faribault, the local newspaper, the *Central Republican*, voiced a virulent anti-Indian view that matched Swisshelm's. The editor, Orville Brown, came from Jefferson County, the same remote segment of upstate New York as Whipple, but there the resemblance ended. A radical Republican, Brown regularly flayed the Lincoln administration for what he regarded as a pitiful lack of ruthlessness in prosecuting the war against secessionist "pirates." He demanded emancipation of slaves in the spring of 1861 to undermine the South.[9] And he editorialized with bedrock certainty that subversive Southerners had instigated the Dakota War. He ranked the Indians as "inhuman barbarians" (August 27) and deemed them fit for "total extermination" (September 3). And he made it clear that he meant fate ought to be brought to bear "not only of the Sioux tribe but all other Indian tribes in the State."

Brown maintained a fury so intense he worked his exterminationist rhetoric even into editorials that did not deal with the Dakota War. Nor could the editor resist twisting the knife when contrasting the war's brutality with the preaching of Christian missions to the Dakotas. Like Senator Wilkinson in his dismissive letter to Whipple in April 1862, Brown discounted any value that the Dakotas received from missionaries in their thirty years among the tribe. Writing on October 15, he jeered at reports that some Dakotas belonged to a peace party or had come willingly into Colonel Sibley's camp. He liked sweeping statements. "For more than 250 years, Christians have been wasting in fruitless efforts to Christianize American heathens; during that time thousands of them have been brought in contact with civilization and Christianity. They have in all their wars with white men learned that their women and children were exempt from its horrors, were spared from murder and rapine; but here the outbreak begins right around a Christian Mission, and weak and defenseless women are selected as the victims on whom they would exhibit their refinement in cruelty and their proficiency in savage ferocity and brutal barbarity."[10]

Whipple resisted replying. Instead, he told Senator Henry Rice that he would keep the focus on his ideas rather than risk making the debate personal. If he asked for much more than reform of the Indian office, those who suspected him of being too close to the Indians would harry him with tireless hostility. "It would only call down a pack of harpies and do no good,"[11] he wrote. So, Whipple asked Minnesotans to search their consciences. In "The Duty of Citizens," he reached beyond the call for reform to request a singularly difficult task in a time of such outrage: moral introspection. He called the war experienced by Minnesota's civilians by its accepted name, a "massacre," and he expressed no wonder that the state's whites wanted vengeance.

"But if that vengeance is to be more than a savage thirst for blood, we must examine the causes which have brought this bloodshed, that our condemnation fall on the guilty." That sentence reflected the worry that gnawed at Whipple. After he returned to Minnesota, he read a public description of the trials. Written by Rev. Stephen Riggs, it contained the news that the commission had taken no more than seven hours to try and convict more than 10 percent of the total men it condemned.

In sharp contrast to the many Minnesotans who blamed the war on bestial inclinations allegedly natural to the Dakotas, Whipple returned in his document to review what he considered incompetent and dangerous government policy. And in a singular statement to his readers, he flatly rejected the idea that race had anything to do with the violence. "Our white race would not be proof against the corrupt influences which have clustered round these heathen. It would make a Sodom of any civilized community under heaven." Blunt talk about the negative effect they might have on other people was not language nineteenth-century whites usually heard. In "The Duty of Citizens" Whipple also made it clear that he regarded the chief barbarities in the war to have been committed not by traditional Indian chiefs and leaders but rather by opportunists who had always been good at playing both sides of the street. "The leaders of the massacre were men who have always been the pliant tools of white men."

As for penalties against those who had led the war, Whipple stated unequivocally that citizens had a "clear right to ask our rulers to punish the guilty." That reasoning was as much biblical as it was secular. But he also called attention to—and, in some cases, named in his text—the Dakotas who had intervened to save whites. "Are we to reward their fidelity by a cry of extermination?

"As one whose life must be spent in Minnesota, whose home cannot be changed at will, whose lot for good or ill must be identified with her weal or woe, I feel a deep solicitude that our settlement of this war shall be such as to call down the blessing of God. The nation cannot afford to be unjust." His final words, in a foretaste of what lay shortly ahead, noted that he had heard calls for exiling the state's Indians. He reminded people that the tribes had been moved repeatedly, through treaties, and in such actions they had felt the force of broken government promises. If the Dakotas were removed from Minnesota, he said, it must be done in as constructive a manner as possible. "[W]e ought to see that our nation does its whole duty, that the Indians shall have a strong government, an individual right in the soil, a just system of trade, a wise system of civilization, and honest agents."[12]

Whipple replied at least once to his critics. In a letter to the editor of the *Saint Paul Pioneer*, he protested "a misapprehension of the object of my appeal." Before the war, he had not wanted to be thought "an alarmist" about a possible Indian war; he had devoted his energies to demanding reform among "those alone who had it in their power to effect it." But he remained troubled about the military tribunals. Riggs had said the commission condemned upwards of thirty Indians in hearings that lasted no more than seven hours. "It left a very painful impression on my mind," he said, "and for the sake of all parties concerned I called attention to it." He again asked the state's citizens to join him in his work for reform. "There is little which brings hope to the patriot and Christian save his abiding faith in Almighty God. That faith demands such open handed and impartial justice as will vindicate us before the world."[13] Whipple thought in a very broad perspective.

Three days after publication of Whipple's essay, Lincoln made his decision about the executions. On December 6, Lincoln said that he had reviewed the trial records and found evidence in only thirty-nine cases that would warrant capital punishment. There were two grounds for such a sentence, both involving extreme crimes committed under cover of war: murder or rape of civilians. Lincoln did not include on the list the names of the Dakota men on whose behalf Riggs had appealed to the president. Lincoln included almost no other commentary on his decision, but it was clear that he had come down on mercy's side. He would spare 87 percent of the convicted Dakotas.[14]

In a note accompanying the list of names, Lincoln asked Sibley to hang the convicted men within two weeks, on Friday, December 19. Sibley telegraphed back and asked for a week's extension to make preparations that, he said, were necessary to preserve public order. He said he wanted to protect the Dakotas who would not be executed. As others had done in the previous month, Sibley warned Lincoln that Minnesota did not lack ready recruits for lynch mobs. If angry citizens could swarm a caravan made up largely of Dakota women and children at New Ulm a month before, then certainly there existed plenty of people ready to break the Indians out of their prison quarters in Mankato and take them to the nearest tree or simply shoot or knife them on the spot. "The excitement prevails in all sections of the state and secret combinations exist embracing thousands of citizens pledged to execute all the Indians," Sibley wrote. "Matters must be managed with great discretion and as much secrecy as possible to prevent a fearful collision between the U.S. forces and the Citizens."[15] Within military ranks, Sibley knew he had men who would be only too happy to see the Indians hanged. On December 15, he received a brief letter from an army sergeant, Frank Gauthier, volunteering his services as hangman. "[I]n case you should be trouble to find anyone to hung them I offer you my Service and I warranted you to hung well."[16] Sibley moved the execution date to Friday, December 26. Thirty-eight men would hang—after issuing his original order, Lincoln had lowered the number by one, commuting a death sentence on the testimony of the missionary Thomas Williamson, who personally investigated the man's case and argued for his innocence of war crimes.[17]

Dissatisfied by Lincoln's decision, Minnesota's political leaders moved swiftly to exact a further measure of rough justice. On December 16, Senator Morton Wilkinson and Representative William Windom introduced bills in the Senate and House, respectively, to remove the Dakota and Winnebago tribes from the state. The legislation would amount to an ethnic cleansing of the state's southern half. That the Winnebagos were included was remarkable. Except for a few individuals, the tribe had taken no part in the war. They had already been moved more than once, from their traditional grounds in Wisconsin, but the reservation they had been given in southern Minnesota contained fertile land and also sat in close proximity to Mankato.[18]

The next day, the *Saint Paul Pioneer* published another essay by Whipple, which again appealed to the spirit of reason and focused in part on the question of exile. He titled his public letter "What Shall We Do with the Indians?" The bishop noted that he had been charged with "sympathy with savage crimes" for his writings, but the new letter made clear he would not give up his campaign to sway public opinion. "Experience has taught that in a republic the only time to secure a needed reform is when the people feel its necessity."[19] He disagreed with the "unanimous" cry for driving the Dakotas into exile; he proposed two alternatives. He asked that people acknowledge that Indians had saved whites and those men and women should be separated from those who had backed the war; the peace party should be rewarded with homes. He also pled that, if the other Dakotas were to be exiled, their future should be more than mere punishment, that their homeland should be a site "carefully selected, on account of its adaptation to their wants and its fitness to foster civilization."[20] He did not want the Indians dumped out on the High Plains. Instead, he still wanted what he had always sought: a fertile land that would be conducive to agriculture and a settled way of life. He wanted the Dakotas to have a government appropriate for this way of living, with laws plainly stated that would be enforced by federal officials, for the benefit both of the Indians and their white neighbors. He wanted housing, farming implements, and schools. Yes, it would cost money to do this, but the bishop emphatically said that expense would amount to far less than the devastation inflicted by another war. The letter, plainly written, appealed directly to people's consciences—provided, of course, they still could hear them.

In the week remaining before the hanging, action shifted to the prison in which the condemned Dakotas were held in Mankato. A handful of missionaries worked among the men, in particular, Rev. Augustin Ravoux, a Roman Catholic priest who later claimed to have baptized the majority of those under death sentences. The conversions later spread among the large group of prisoners remaining in Mankato.[21]

The mass execution took place, as planned, the morning after Christmas. More than a thousand soldiers stood guard, acting as a protective cordon between the gallows and the thousands of civilians who had come to look on. Infantry ranks, two soldiers deep, surrounded the site. Mounted cavalrymen sat their horses behind the foot soldiers. An artist working for *Frank Leslie's Illustrated Newspaper*, a national publication, captured the scene. The condemned Dakotas shared a broad platform raised high enough so that their bodies could fall freely once the trapdoors beneath them had been sprung. The ropes would arrest their fall, breaking thirty-eight necks simultaneously. The gallows stood at a height, too, to allow the public a clear view of the execution.

One witness to the scene, Julius Owens, a fourteen-year-old whose family lived in Freeborn County, bordering Iowa, later recalled helping transport groups of soldiers to and from Mankato in his family's horse-drawn wagon in the days before the execution. On the 26th, he reached town just before the hanging. Seventy-one years later, he wrote up his recollections of that morning. "The Indians were brought out accompanied by a Catholic priest, and by means of a step-ladder ascended to the platform. Some of the Indians were singing, while others were smoking cigars as they walked up the steps and around the platform to their places. Ropes were placed around their necks, caps were pulled down over their faces, their elbows tied behind their backs and their wrists fastened in front of them.

"When everything was ready," Owens said, "a man whose family had all been killed by the Indians, stood with an ax in his hand to cut the big cable at the sounding of three taps of the drum. The signal was given, the waiting man severed the rope and all the Indians fell at once." Owens saw the rope of one among those executed break at the end of the man's fall. Soldiers carried the man back up the gallows, put another noose around his neck, and let him fall again. Local doctors then moved in to examine the bodies. Owens continued his narrative: "After the physicians pronounced the Indians dead, big government wagons drawn by six mules were brought to the scaffold. A soldier taking hold of either side of the bodies, while a third soldier cut the ropes which held them. The bodies were then placed in the wagons and carried to one long trench prepared for them."[22]

Seven years after Owens set down his memories, a newspaper reporter in Beaverton, Oregon, tracked down an eighty-eight-year-old resident named Marcia Doughty Pike, another witness to the execution. She had stood in the crowd in Mankato as a curious ten-year-old that December 26 and watched the bodies drop. The passage of three-quarters of a century had not eased her outrage, either over the war or at those like Whipple who had urged a path other than revenge. She told her interviewer that the Dakotas had behaved as "monsters," but that "people far removed from the scenes of their inhuman butcheries" found them sympathetic. "President Lincoln was importuned beyond all reasonable bounds" on behalf of the 303 originally condemned. Pike also recalled that the civilian spectators, watching the 38 men drop to their deaths, "could not repress a shout of righteous exultation."[23]

In a grim aftermath to the execution, the mass grave was desecrated within hours. Amateur gravediggers, armed with shovels, came after the bodies that night. By the next morning, the corpses were gone. What happened to them? Twenty-five years to the day after the executions, a man named John Meagher sent what he called a "relic" to the secretary of the Minnesota Historical Society. In a cover letter, Meagher said he had accompanied a local doctor and "a few well known men" in taking a horse team and wagon to the burial site. They were going to help the doctor find corpses for dissection. But some in the group had also been friends of George Gleason, who had been killed the first day of the war, shot down in his wagon as he attempted to drive Sarah Wakefield and her children to safety. Digging into the graves, Meagher's companions found the body of the man they believed killed Gleason. "We all felt keenly the injury [he] had don[e] in murdering our old friend Gleason, in cold blood." They cut off a braid of the corpse's hair "with the intention of sending it to Gleason's relatives." Meagher said the hair was made into a watch chain "by a Lady friend in St. Paul." He later sent it to the Minnesota Historical Society, "thinking that some day it might be of interest with the other momentoes of those terrible times and that great hanging Event."[24]

Whipple did not reach Mankato in time to witness the hanging. He got to the city the next day and preached there a day later, on Sunday the 28th. Despite the illustration on Frank Leslie's cover, the attention of many in the Union had been drawn back to the Civil War's main theater. During a four-day period, ending December 15, the Army of the Potomac had suffered an enormous defeat at Fredericksburg, Virginia. Attacking through that town, beside the Rappahannock River, Major General Ambrose Burnside urged his men uphill against entrenched Confederate forces. He took 12,600 casualties. A London *Times* correspondent, writing after the battle, described a scene in which "lying so close to each other that you might step from body to body, lay acres of the Federal dead."[25] The First Minnesota Volunteers took part in the fighting but were spared being ordered directly into the slaughter. A soldier in the regiment later quoted its commander, General Alfred Sully, as having said, though he risked a court-martial, "I was not going to murder my men."[26]

Given both local and national events, Whipple's choice of scripture on which to preach that Sunday seemed peculiarly apt. His text described a dialogue between two enemies during the civil war that divided biblical Israel's houses of David and Saul. "Then Abner called to Joab, and said, Shall the sword devour for ever? Knowest thou not that it will be bitterness in the latter end?" (2 Sam. 2:26).

Whipple had never been a pacifist and his experiences neither among wounded civilians in Saint Peters nor among the dead and injured at Antietam had made him one. He came to Mankato not to condemn war. He briefly described the ravages of the battlefield, as he had personally seen them. He knew that some in his congregation that morning had had intimate experience of the horrors in the Dakota War. "I have no mawkish fear of war; there are times when there is no help for it," he said. Politically, Whipple stood firmly in the Union camp. Theologically, he unquestioningly rejected rebellion against government—especially legally constituted government—as an offense against what God had established. But unlike many Northern clergymen who claimed God's favor for the North, he did not take such a parochial stand. He could not, because he believed that both sides were guilty of sin, and God would be the ultimate arbiter, not a soldier fighting for either side.

"It seems like a troubled nightmare dream. Both sides not only claiming justice but claiming before God and man that they are fighting for all that men hold dear for home, kindred, and country."[27]

Whipple's words echo the language Lincoln had used—the Lincoln who had written "Meditation on the Divine Will" earlier that year—and would use again in his second inaugural address. The two men shared an appreciation of God's sovereignty. God stood beyond human reckoning. As Lincoln would say at his second inaugural more than two years hence, "The Almighty has his own purposes." God was unknowable. Whipple drew from his reading of the Bible that God was beyond human power but demanded much in obedience and reverence. In his sermon that Sunday, the bishop called on his congregation to temper their anger, to be purposeful but merciful as well—"to fight with no malice in our hearts."[28] He reasoned that God demanded dispassion; mere humans would be God's instruments, and to seek revenge would vitiate the divine demand for justice alone. His sermon followed a familiar track: shun sin and obey God.

Whipple had another point to make. However much rebellion displeased God, the divine judgment could be provoked by another "dark sin." Here the bishop referred to "the wicked neglect and robbery of the poor whom the providence of God has made our wards." He spoke not of "the poor" in general but of the two groups who had endured such terrible mistreatment as to stir God's wrath. "The one portion of our land has fostered a system which destroyed the sanctity of home, which made a mock of marriage, which broke up the kindred which God made holy." Whipple had toured the South as a young man and voiced his loathing of slave sales. His congregation understood him to be referring to that subject. But rather than allow the people before him—deep in the antislavery North—to feel comfortable in their morality, the bishop also located the sin God hated as existing in another system close to home. "In the other section, we have looked unconcerned at the iniquity and fraud of an Indian system which we knew was a reproach to a Christian nation. We had forgotten that God is not blind, that the comfortless sighing of the needy will reach his ear."[29]

Mistreatment of Native Americans—unfair treaties, sales of whiskey, the deposing of their rightful chiefs, the denial of promises for their development—could be classified with slavery. Whipple did not record how his congregation reacted to this proposition, but he kept saying it. Mankato simply marked the first stop on a pastoral tour he took through Minnesota during the next seven weeks. He preached the sermon twenty-five more times, including at Saint Peter, on the Minnesota River, where he had served as Asa Daniels's assistant in the makeshift hospital only four months earlier. On January 16, 1863, he preached it in Saint Cloud, where Jane Swisshelm—lately departed for Washington—had published her editorials demanding Indian extermination.

Whipple had some evidence that he had reached a few people. He received a letter from a man who lived in Mankato, thanking him for his work. "I honor you for the moral courage exhibited in boldly presenting the truth at a time when it is unpalatable," wrote William Marshall. "I am satisfied that if the Indians had been dealt with justly, there would have been no outbreak—no bloody blackened devastation and desolation of the fair borders of our state."[30]

Ten

Exile and Community

HANGING THIRTY-EIGHT MEN IN MANKATO, MINNE-
sota, did not bring peace. Nor did it diminish Henry Whipple's
passion for Indian rights. Even before the trapdoor sprang open
and hurtled the condemned men to their deaths, Minnesota's
political leaders began to press hard for exiling the survivors
beyond the state, out onto the Great Plains. Within days of
President Lincoln's announcement to spare nearly 90 percent of
those originally scheduled for death, bills were introduced into
the Senate and House to strip the Dakotas and the peaceful
Winnebagos of their reservations in Minnesota. Thousands of
members of both tribes would be sent west, by steamship and
train.

Before either bill could be enacted, Whipple began working on ways to mitigate their effects. Unsurprisingly, he had
emerged from his experience advocating for Indian rights better
known—and not simply in Minnesota. Within little more than
a year, he returned to Washington, this second visit on behalf of
the Ojibwes; he would again meet with Lincoln.

As Congress opened discussions on removing Minnesota's
Indians from their historic homeland, many Dakotas began
converting to Christianity. Some of those who went into exile

did so singing hymns from the decks of the steamboats bearing them down the Mississippi River. From descriptions of the public hostility with which the exiles were treated, their new faith did little to persuade many white Minnesotans that they might share a fundamental basis for living together.

Lincoln's decision about who would be hanged for war crimes left three groups of Dakotas, totaling about two thousand people, under military authority. The two smallest groups were housed in the prison in Mankato, more than three hundred men in all. They included the thirty-eight to be hanged and the much larger group whose death sentences Lincoln had commuted. Another seventeen hundred Dakotas—mainly women and children—were confined in Fort Snelling, outside Saint Paul. That larger group, peaceful individuals who faced no charges, had been taken into military custody after the captives had been turned over to Sibley, now a general, at Camp Release. Their detention could be attributed in part to their protection, as threats continued to be made against all Dakotas in Minnesota by aggrieved whites who viewed members of the tribe without distinction. In both locations, a small number of Christian missionaries set up makeshift classrooms that taught the confined Indians to read and write and also preached them the gospel.[1]

Besides their jailors, the condemned men were exposed to Protestants like Rev. Stephen Riggs and Rev. Thomas Williamson, and the French-born Jesuit priest Rev. Augustin Ravoux. In the midst of the trauma these Dakotas had experienced—a losing war, confinement by federal troops, and separation from their families—they embraced a spiritual expression that the vast majority of the tribe had until recently resisted. Among the men condemned to die, a majority chose baptism from Ravoux, who had been active in Minnesota and the surrounding region since 1840—nearly as long as Riggs and Williamson. Ravoux would later say he had baptized thirty-three of the men executed. He had accompanied the group to the scaffold.[2]

But in the weeks to come, Riggs played a major role in pros-
elytizing and also publicizing the mission work through the
Boston-based organization to which he belonged, the American
Board of Commissioners of Foreign Missions. The organization,
founded in 1810 by graduates of Williams College, brought together Congregationalists and Presbyterians. It worked to convert Native Americans as well as overseas populations. The
effectiveness of its work only began to become apparent early
in 1863, when missionaries reported that hundreds of Dakotas in the Fort Snelling camp began attending services.[3] Samuel
Hinman, Whipple's protégé, ever loyal to the Dakotas, worked
intensively among the men, women, and children in Fort Snelling. Eventually, he and Whipple baptized about a hundred. But
Hinman also paid for his attentiveness. One evening a group
of white marauders invaded the camp and singled him out for
attack, beating him into unconsciousness. Even with the Dakotas largely confined, hatred of Indians and all those regarded as
their sympathizers ran dangerously high.[4]

The conversions proved more lasting than the desperate
circumstances in which they occurred, eventually creating a
substantial population of Christianized Dakotas where none
had previously existed. The scholar of religious studies Jennifer Graber has said that some of the American Board–affiliated
missionaries came to see the conversions as products of God's
decision to use warfare and confinement to transform the Dakotas spiritually.[5] An individual description of the conversions'
aftermath would be offered later from Ohiyesa (Charles Eastman), a Dakota separated from much of his family as a child
during the war. His father, whose death sentence was commuted
by Lincoln, underwent baptism from Riggs. Later, the father
sought his youngest son out and introduced him to Christianity.

Whipple visited the Dakotas in the camp at Fort Snelling
weekly. Hinman, no longer on the reservation, continued work
as a missionary there. Whipple estimated later that, thanks to his

efforts, he had confirmed about one hundred in the camp into the Episcopal Church, but on one occasion when he brought his new parishioners Communion, the bishop excited a sensational rebuke from a newspaper editor, who wrote a highly opinionated piece accusing him of "sacrilege" and of giving the church's "holiest rites" to "red-handed murderers." Whipple seethed over the accusation—but not for long, as he encountered the writer on the sidewalk a few days later and declared to the man that he would not put up with "lying." The two men managed to reach an understanding, and the newspaper refrained from such criticisms from then on.[6]

Whipple faced a far more difficult challenge: the political pressure that had been steadily building within Minnesota to send the Dakotas into permanent exile. On a political level, the move began ten days before the executions, when two members of the state's congressional delegation—Senator Wilkinson and Representative Windom—introduced bills that would require the military to remove the Dakota and Winnebago tribes from the state. (For the Winnebagos, who had not taken part in the war, the move from their reservation south of Mankato would be their fourth, having been twice previously uprooted from reservations in Wisconsin and eastern Minnesota.) Congress approved the measures early in March 1863. Both tribes were to be moved to a remote location in Dakota Territory. The army waited until spring. In April, the Indians reprieved by Lincoln were removed from Mankato, shackled, and put aboard a steamboat bound down the Minnesota River to Saint Paul. From there, they were shipped down the Mississippi to a military camp in Davenport, Iowa.

The legislation also called for the Dakotas at Fort Snelling to be deported. Scores had died during a harsh and hungry winter, but a population of more than 1,450 remained. On May 4, nearly 800 Indians were crowded aboard the steamship *Davenport* for transport to Missouri. The boat stopped briefly at Saint Paul, remaining long enough for a mob to collect and throw stones at the Indians, who were at the time holding a religious service. Several were injured. The next day, a second group of Dakotas were taken aboard the *Northerner*. The *Davenport* took its charges to Saint Louis and placed them aboard the *Florence*, another steamship, to transport them up the Missouri River. The *Northerner* disgorged its passengers in Hannibal, Missouri, where they were packed into rail freight cars and taken like cattle across the state. The two groups were reunited on May 17, when they were packed aboard the *Florence* and taken eight hundred miles up the river to a place called Crow Creek. Thirteen people died in the crowded and unsanitary conditions prevailing en route.[7]

After the Dakotas, the Winnebagos followed. By the end of June, the tribes (who did not get along) had been located on Crow Creek—nearly 3,300 men, women, and children. The area proved a poor one for an agricultural lifestyle. Again, scores of Indians died. Within the next three years, the government relocated both tribes to separate reservations in Nebraska. Hinman, who had gone with the Dakotas, unsurprisingly found the tribe's treatment disgraceful. Ordinarily a gentle man, he wrote to Whipple saying that, were he an Indian, he would make war on whites.[8]

Before the Dakotas' exile, Whipple approached Henry Sibley to plead mercy for the families of men and women who had avoided warfare and been active in the Dakotas' peace efforts that had saved whites and captives of mixed heritage. The bishop also asked Sibley not to allow the deportation of the wives and children of Dakota men who would serve the army as scouts on a military expedition planned for that summer. Whipple found Sibley sympathetic, but the general declared himself bound by the new laws to remove all the Dakotas to Crow Creek. Whipple's partial solution was to ask Sibley if he might take some Indian families to Faribault, where he

and Alexander Faribault could settle them on some of the latter's land. The idea bore fruit, in that Whipple and Faribault
were able to establish a village of Dakotas on about twenty
acres of Faribault's land. Faribault himself, the well-off son of
a fur trader, eventually spent $4,000 to help feed and clothe
them. Symbolically then, Whipple was able to extend to several Dakota families the very hospitality that he had originally
been shown in Faribault. He had been elected bishop when the
church in Minnesota lacked any official residence for him. In
1859, Whipple had a title but no house; he had located the seat
of his diocese in Faribault because that is where citizens offered
him land and money to help build it.[9]

The bishop would praise Alexander Faribault as "one of
the kindest men I have ever known." But, inevitably, their im-
provised move on behalf of the Dakota families outraged local
citizens who did not want Indians—even those associated
with the peace party—in their midst. Whipple dismissed the
complaints as "much excitement" and "foolish threats," but
the anger deeply stung at least some of the Dakotas, who had
risked much to save white Christians. Among these Dakotas,
there was no one more eloquent than Taopi, a Christianized
Indian who had led the agricultural faction among the Mdewakantons before the Dakota War. Sibley had praised him for his
work in rescuing captives at the war's end and had given him
a written note, identifying him as "entitled to the everlasting
gratitude of the American people" for having helped save what
the general estimated were two hundred people. But in the
period after the war, Faribault wrote a public letter on Taopi's behalf, recording the Indian as telling him he had been
threatened. "Tell them not to shoot me like a dog but to send
for me to go to the public square and I can show them how a
man can die." The settlement never rose above being a small
and imperfect response to the mass exile; the Dakotas living
on Faribault's land received no federal aid and lived in pov-

erty. Still, the community, on a bluff above the Straight River, lasted thirty years.[10]

In the summer of 1863, the army resumed its campaign against the Dakotas who had fled with Little Crow onto the western plains. Both Sibley and General Alfred Sully, a former colonel in the First Minnesota Volunteers, led columns into Dakota Territory to continue the battles of the previous summer. In late July, Sibley encountered and fought three times with hunting parties east of the Missouri Rivers, in what is today central North Dakota. Operating to his south, Sully came upon a camp of Indians in August and mounted an attack when it was not clear that his target was hostile. The action, at a place called Whitestone Hill, disgusted one of his interpreters—Samuel Brown, a son of Joseph Brown, who had served as Dakota Indian agent under President Buchanan. The younger Brown wrote his father to say that Sully had nothing about which to boast as his attack had been carried out largely against women and children and ought to be regarded as "a perfect massacre."[11]

The military encounters west of Minnesota overlapped a pathetic—and fatal—incident within the state. On July 3, Nathan and Chauncey Lampson, a father and son, sighted two Indians gathering berries near Hutchinson, about two dozen miles southeast of Acton, where the Dakota War had begun nearly a year earlier. The two pairs exchanged gunfire, leaving one of the Indians mortally wounded and the elder Lampson injured. Later that day, local whites recovered the body of the Dakota man, and scalped and mutilated the corpse. Later that month, the dead man's son conclusively identified the body as that of Little Crow. The adolescent, Wowinape, had been captured by Sibley's forces. He had been with his father in the berry field and was tried by a military commission and sentenced to hang. The order was never carried out and Wowinape was eventually released. He later took the name Thomas Wakeman, became an ordained minister, and founded the first YMCA chapter among the Dakotas. Nathan Lampson received a state bounty of five hundred dollars for Little Crow's scalp.[12]

That year, too, Senator Rice, who had long been sympathetic to Whipple, recommended the bishop serve on a commission that would oversee distribution of annuities to the Ojibwes, in return for a new federal treaty with the tribe. But the appointment never worked out. Whipple later said he was unable to carry out the duties partly because he had been injured in a fall from his wagon, but he also complained to federal officials that the commission had been forced to work in the dark, never receiving adequate information on the annuity payment nor being solicited as to an opinion on whether the treaty's terms were actually being honored. Late in the year, the bishop opened his door to a prominent Ojibwe, named Madwaganonint, who had trekked more than a hundred miles through the snow to ask his help. The Indian said he had never signed the treaty, as it provided no cattle, no horses, and no food to the tribe. The injustice struck Whipple as plain. The bishop decided to travel again to Washington, with Madwaganonint and other Red Lake chiefs, to renegotiate the treaty.[13]

In April 1864, Whipple saw Lincoln again, albeit under less urgent circumstances than on the first occasion. In Washington, the bishop remained closely identified with his demand for reform of government dealings with the Indians. Edwin Stanton, Lincoln's secretary of war, told Whipple's cousin, Henry Halleck, that if the bishop had come all the way to tell them about corruption in the Indian office, they already knew about it. But he also offered some advice that Whipple found worthy of recording: "[T]he government never reforms an evil until the people demand it." Halleck relayed Stanton's advice that "the Indian will be saved" once the bishop found a way to reach "the heart of the American people."[14]

Lincoln wrote out a note, sending Whipple on to see Representative Windom. It may have seemed less than a useful connection, given Windom's role in writing legislation in December 1862 that put the Dakotas into exile. Later, public opinion would begin to move, in part because of a catastrophic campaign in Colorado against Indians friendly to the United States. In November 1864, a force of seven hundred Colorado militia led by John Chivington, a colonel and Methodist minister, had descended upon a small camp of Cheyenne and Arapaho Indians at Sand Creek and perpetrated a massacre of extreme cruelty, including the deliberate killing of women and children and the mutilation of corpses. The atrocities shocked the public. The butchery at Sand Creek echoed the worst charges laid against the Dakotas, amounting to a national scandal that led to a congressional investigation. Whipple was out of the country at the time, but he made sure to include a lengthy report of it in his autobiography.[15]

Whipple spent two weeks in Washington with the Ojibwe chiefs. At one point, Lincoln found time to show the Indians around the White House, but the process of renegotiating the treaty proved to be difficult going. The bishop had testy moments with William Dole, commissioner of the Office of Indian Affairs. "I came here as an honest man to put you in possession of facts to save another outbreak," Whipple told him, in words laden with meaning for anyone who remembered the devastation of the Dakota War. "I am going home, and when you next hear from me it will be through the public press." Whipple did succeed in getting changes made, but only after Dole had spoken to Senator Rice, who warned him that the bishop meant business. Whipple would recall the episode as "one of the severest personal conflicts I have had in my life."[16]

Later in the year, Episcopalians in Minnesota urged Whipple to take a sabbatical, for health reasons. He did so, journeying with his friend Robert Minturn to London that fall. In the winter, he accepted Minturn's generosity and traveled on to Palestine, a trip that moved him spiritually but almost killed him too. Whipple contracted what he called a "Syrian fever" and only gradually returned to health, nursed by friends there and later, when the illness returned, in France. He did not get back to the United States until April 1865, after Lincoln's assassination.[17]

In Washington, especially under Lincoln's successor but one, Ulysses Grant, political thinking about Native Americans began to change somewhat. Over the coming years, Whipple would be consulted for his ideas, but the government also pursued a military policy that led the army into continuing confrontations with the Dakotas and their affiliated bands, the Lakotas. Whipple spent relatively little time describing those encounters in his autobiography. His first meeting with Lincoln had been a momentous occasion and his project—trying to obtain justice for Native Americans through sweeping government reform during the Civil War—the most complicated.

In his memoirs, the bishop dwelt often on the peaceful times he had spent among the Dakotas and Ojibwes. When he wrote about his experiences with Madwaganonint in 1863–64, he offered one of the gentlest descriptions of the pleasures he took in his office. Becoming bishop of Minnesota had put him in a difficult position in his first years there, but he gained immensely through friendships and experiences on the frontier, as he never would have in his previous postings as a priest in Chicago or upstate New York. "Nothing lingers longer in the memory than the nights spent around the Indian camp-fire," Whipple wrote. "There, in the heart of primeval nature, under the subtle influences of the ever-shining stars and the murmur of fragrant pines, we have been able to draw forth the legends and traditions of the Indians as we could have done in no other way.

"At night, when the Indians have come into camp, and supper has been followed by prayers, we have rolled ourselves in our blankets round the fire and I have suggested that each one should tell a story, saying I will begin, my white brother will follow, and then our red brothers shall tell a legend of their fathers."[18]

In those moments under the stars, the bishop may have found himself drifting back in spirit to the evenings he spent as a young guest at Peter Doxtater's farmhouse in Adams, New York, listening by the fireside to a very old man tell about his rich, long-ago experiences among another tribe, one that had treated him with great kindness.

Henry Benjamin Whipple, circa 1898

Conclusion

THE EPISCOPAL CHURCH MAINTAINS A LITURGICAL
calendar of men and women whose lives, it has been decided,
have been distinguished by heroic virtue. Taken together, individuals named in these "lesser feast" days are admirably far-
reaching, a net whose breadth includes William Wilberforce,
the great British combatant against slavery; Elizabeth Seton, a
Catholic who founded the Sisters of Charity; and Roger Williams, a Baptist who defiantly pushed the cause of religious
freedom in Puritan New England. The list also names at least
one person known for a single, breathtaking act of self-sacrifice:
Jonathan Daniels, a seminarian and Civil Rights volunteer, who
shoved an adolescent black girl away from the barrel of a shotgun wielded by an Alabama official and took the lethal bullet
himself.

Notably, the church's calendar also names three clergymen
close to Henry Whipple: Bishop Jackson Kemper, whose western missionary diocese included Minnesota until Whipple's
election; Rev. James Breck, who began the church's work in
Minnesota Territory, founding schools and a seminary; and, of
course, Rev. Enmegahbowh, the church's first Native American
deacon, whom Whipple elevated to the priesthood.

That Whipple himself is not among them on the calendar is a source of some debate in the state he made his home. During my travels, I met at least one priest who said he would eventually bring Whipple's cause before the church. But another told me he disagreed; he admired Whipple but thought him too moderate in pursuing his great, abiding conviction.

It is a mark of Bishop Whipple's enduring relevance that he could divide people even now, more than a century after his death in 1901. He is a focus of controversy in academic circles, too, where the figure of a missionary bishop is regarded with suspicion as someone whose attitudes fall short of a religiously pluralistic ideal. Whipple saw the Indians' future as an integrationist would. Yet in the very respect he extended to Native Americans, as people of inherent worth and dignity, he was a man ahead of his time—even if he does not necessarily belong to ours. He continues to surprise. At age twenty-one, on a long sojourn through the South, he expressed a hatred of slavery, not because he held to an ideal of natural liberty but because he believed in the sacred integrity of slave families—husbands, wives, and children. This was at a time when not a single state in the country recognized the legality of slave marriages.

How do we appreciate him now, this small-town New Yorker who made his mark on the frontier, where he became so deeply engaged in a cause so unpopular within his region? Whipple should be measured by his consistency and dedication to a humanitarian cause. He looked in the faces of Native Americans—the subjects of a brutal racism inbred in so many Americans—and he saw men and women as admirable as any others he had known, and very possibly more so. He knew this opened him up to all manner of unpleasant accusations of naïveté, and worse, somehow betraying the interests of white America. But he persisted.

Whipple got to Lincoln before anyone else did and so was able to explain the war to the president in terms of the historic injustice of white–Indian relations. He rejected the spurious accusations common in Minnesota, that the Indians were naturally dangerous. Instead, he focused on their long mistreatment by a government that could, Whipple believed, reform itself and offer them protection, to the benefit of all—and to the pleasure of God.

Did his appeal count when it really mattered, ten or so weeks later, when Lincoln had to decide whether to accept his army's recommendation that more than three hundred men be hanged as punishment for a short, terrible war? Lincoln never said so. But it is difficult to imagine that Whipple's visit did not count in the president's decision. The bishop provided an explanation for what had happened, at least in general terms. When it came time to render judgment, Lincoln reprieved nearly nine of every ten men condemned by the military court.

In Whipple's absence, would no more than thirty-eight have mounted that scaffold in Mankato, to fall in what remains the largest mass execution in American history? Or did Lincoln's meeting with Whipple lead him to spare others from death—five or ten or even fifty? Any number matters, profoundly. Two years after the execution, Whipple traveled through Palestine, spending weeks in Jerusalem. Had he entered into conversation with any learned rabbi about matters of life and death, particularly as it involved intervening to preserve the living, there he could have heard an ancient and affirming declaration from a fundamental text of Jewish law. As regards actions like the one in which he had participated, the Talmud states that whoever saves one life, it is as if he has saved the whole world.

Of how many of us can such a thing be said?

Acknowledgments

IN RESEARCHING THIS BOOK, I OWE GREAT THANKS TO the patient and dedicated men and women working in the libraries and historical societies of which I made use. That list includes the Cornell University Library, Oberlin College Library, Houghton Library at Harvard University and, of course, Byrd Library at Syracuse University. I am grateful, too, for having been allowed liberal use of the South Jefferson Historical Association in Adams, New York; the historical collections of the Episcopal Diocese of Central New York; the Blue Earth County Historical Society in Mankato, Minnesota; the Brown County Historical Society in New Ulm, Minnesota; and the Rice County Historical Society and the Episcopal Cathedral of Our Merciful Savior, both in Faribault, Minnesota.

Above all, however, I extend my deepest gratitude to the women and men at the Minnesota Historical Society in Saint Paul. Their technical help and guidance, delivered with care and unfailing good cheer, did a great deal in encouraging me in my work.

Several people read and helpfully commented on portions of early drafts. I owe a debt of thanks to Gary Clayton Anderson, Phil Arnold, Elisabeth Lasch-Quinn and Mike Flamm. Two

Episcopal Church priests in Minnesota—Rev. James Zotalis and Rev. Ben Scott—were helpful in avidly discussing Whipple with me and looking over a part of my research.

Mark Tauber at HarperCollins gave me early and important encouragement in pursuing this project. My editor, Mickey Maudlin at HarperOne, offered incisive critiques at the time I needed them most. I express my sincere thanks to him. I would be remiss if I did not mention how much I appreciated working with Noël Chrisman and Kathryn Renz in the project's final stages. And looking back to the book's beginnings, I owe my great thanks to my agent, Kris Dahl.

Throughout the process of research and writing, I have been exceptionally fortunate to enjoy support and encouragement from my wonderful wife, Margaret, to whom this book is dedicated.

Notes

Note: *"MHS" refers to the Minnesota Historical Society.*

INTRODUCTION
1. Rev. Dr. Martin Luther King Jr.'s "Letter from a Birmingham Jail" may be found at numerous websites, including www.africa.upenn.edu/Articles_Gen/Letter_Birmingham.html.
2. King, "Letter from a Birmingham Jail."

PROLOGUE: WAITING FOR LINCOLN
1. Henry Whipple, *Lights and Shadows of a Long Episcopate: Being Reminiscences and Recollections of the Right Reverend Henry Benjamin Whipple, D.D., LL.D.* (New York: Macmillan, 1912) 105.
2. Michael Burlingame, *Abraham Lincoln: A Life*, vol. 2 (Baltimore: Johns Hopkins University Press, 2008) 407–08. Burlingame quotes from the writings of two cabinet secretaries, Gideon Welles and Samuel P. Chase, both present at the September 22 meeting at which Lincoln revealed his intention to issue the Emancipation Proclamation.
3. Francis Paul Prucha, *The Great Father: The United States Government and the American Indians*, vol. 1 (Lincoln: Univ. of Nebraska, 1984) 293–302; David Nichols, *Lincoln and the Indians: Civil War Policy and Politics* (Columbia: Univ. of Missouri, 1978) 8–10.
4. Whipple, *Lights and Shadows*, 66.
5. Abraham Lincoln, Second Annual Message to Congress, December 1, 1862. The message may be found at several websites, among them www.presidency.ucsb.edu/ws/?pid=29503.
6. Abraham Lincoln, "Reply to Emancipation Memorial Presented by Chicago Christians of All Denominations," *The Collected Works of Abraham Lincoln*, vol. 5 (New Brunswick: Rutgers Univ. Press, 1953) 419–25. Lincoln

concluded the meeting, which took place September 13, 1862, saying, "Whatever shall appear to be God's will I will do."

7. Whipple, *Lights and Shadows*, 525.

8. Whipple, *Lights and Shadows*, 105.

9. Whipple made frequent use of the word "heathen" when speaking of Native Americans. It grates in today's hearing, sounding dismissive, even demeaning. However, to people of Whipple's era and religious calling, the word had a primary theological significance: it identified people outside Western monotheism. A heathen, to a nineteenth-century missionary, meant a human being who did not worship the single God of the Jews, Christians, and Muslims.

10. Henry Halleck to Henry Whipple, letter, October 30, 1841, MHS manuscripts collections.

11. Whipple to Elizabeth Whipple, letter, October 24, 1862, "My lame hand kept me for a long time from writing any letters . . ." MHS manuscripts collections.

12. John Whipple to Henry Whipple, letter, November 13, 1837, MHS manuscripts collection.

13. Whipple, *Lights and Shadows*, 2, 5.

14. Richard Berleth, *Bloody Mohawk: The French and Indian War and American Revolution on New York's Frontier* (Hensonville, NY: Black Dome, 2009) 226.

15. Hamilton Child, *Geographic Gazetteer of Jefferson County* (Syracuse: Syracuse Journal, 1890).

16. Fintan O'Toole, *White Savage: William Johnson and the Invention of America* (New York: Farrar, Straus and Giroux, 2005) 195.

17. Documents describing Doxtater's life, are at the Historical Association of South Jefferson in Adams, N.Y. Typical is this line, from the *South Jefferson Journal*, March 22, 1882: "Taken away at a tender age, Peter survived the hardships of his long journey and was adopted into an Indian family, and became so thoroughly identified with the red men that he forgot his mother tongue and became a thoroughpaced Indian in everything but color."

18. Whipple, *Lights and Shadows*, 30.

19. "Reminiscences of Adams," Historical Association of South Jefferson manuscripts collections, 5–6.

20. "Reminiscences of Adams," 6.

21. Henry Whipple, unpublished manuscript, 15–16, MHS manuscripts collections.

22. Augustus Field Beard, *A History of the American Missionary Association* (Boston: Pilgrim Press, 1910) 207–11.

23. Lester B. Shippee, editor, *Bishop Whipple's Southern Diary 1843–1844* (New York: Da Capo, 1968), 69.

24. Whipple, *Lights and Shadows*, 4–5.

25. Whipple, *Lights and Shadows*, 18.

26. Whipple, personal diary, MHS manuscripts collection.

27. Whipple, *Lights and Shadows*, 19.

28. George Tanner, *Fifty Years of Church Work in the Diocese of Minnesota, 1857–1907* (Saint Paul: Committee on Publication, 1909) 290.
29. Whipple, *Lights and Shadows*, 88–89.
30. Margaret Lucie Thomas, "Enmegahbowh: Native and Christian" (paper for class, Pacific School of Religion, December 16, 1994) 3, accessed at http://archive.episcopalchurch.org/documents/NAM_Enmegahbowh_Native_and_Christian.pdf.
31. Whipple, unpublished manuscript, 15, MHS manuscripts collections.
32. With his wounded hand, Whipple did little writing in September 1862. Unfortunately, that meant he noted neither the date nor day of the week that he met with Lincoln. Whipple later told his friend Rev. Ezekiel Gear that—with Lincoln's written permission—he spent "several days" studying the Dakota treaties in the Office of Indian Affairs. The bishop departed Washington at week's end to visit wounded soldiers at Antietam shortly after hearing news of that battle, leaving me to suspect this meeting occurred on Monday, September 15, the earliest possible time that week.
33. Whipple, unpublished manuscript, 15, MHS manuscripts collections.

One: THE SUNDAY AFTERNOON MURDERS

1. Gary Clayton Anderson and Alan Woolrich, editors, *Through Dakota Eyes: Narrative Accounts of the Minnesota Indian War of 1862* (Saint Paul: Minnesota Historical Society Press, 1988) 35–36.
2. Henry Whipple, *Lights and Shadows of a Long Episcopate: Being Reminiscences and Recollections of the Right Reverend Henry Benjamin Whipple, D.D., LL.D.* (New York: Macmillan, 1912) 514.
3. Whipple, *Lights and Shadows*, 108.
4. Lucian Hubbard and Return Holcome, *Minnesota in Three Centuries*, vol. 3 (Mankato, MN: Publishing Society of Minnesota, 1908) 303; Isaac Heard, *The History of the Sioux War* (New York: Harper & Brothers, 1864) 52.
5. Heard, *History*, 53.
6. Doane Robinson, *A History of the Dakota or Sioux Indians* (Minneapolis: Ross & Haines, 1967) 19.
7. Heard, *History*, 52.
8. William Watts Folwell, *A History of Minnesota*, vol. 2 (Saint Paul: Minnesota Historical Society, 1924) 239; and Kenneth Carley, *The Dakota War of 1862* (Saint Paul: Minnesota Historical Society, 1976) 10. Carley says residents of Rice Creek were "looked down upon" by other Dakota as "troublemakers and malcontents."
9. Folwell, *A History of Minnesota*, 1:254–55.
10. Anderson and Woolrich, *Through Dakota Eyes*, 23–27, 35–36.
11. Folwell, *A History of Minnesota*, 2:240.
12. Heard, *History*, 54–55; Hubbard and Holcome, *Minnesota in Three Centuries*, 3:304.
13. Whipple, *Lights and Shadows*, 43.
14. Robinson, *A History of the Dakota*, 33. Robinson quotes Marquette as praising the Dakota for never breaking a promise.

15. U.S. Department of the Interior, "Ratified Treaty No. 108, Documents Relating to the Negotiation of the Treaty of June 19, 1858, with the Mdwakantons and Wahpekuta Sioux Indians," unnumbered page. The conversation took place on April 9: speaking to William Dole, Commissioner of Indian Affairs, Little Crow said, "Last winter, we were badly off, but it was because, in compliance with your wishes, we went in pursuit of Inkpadutah, and neglected our cornfields."
16. Heard, *History*, 55.
17. Hubbard and Holcombe, *Minnesota in Three Centuries*, 3:309–10.
18. Heard, *History*, 57.
19. Heard, *History*, 57.
20. Whipple, *Lights and Shadows*, 106–7.
21. Henry David Thoreau, *Letters to Various Persons* (Boston: James R. Osgood, 1877) 205.
22. Whipple, *Lights and Shadows*, 107.
23. Gary Clayton Anderson, *Little Crow: Spokesman for the Sioux* (Saint Paul: Minnesota Historical Society, 1986) 81–82, 129.
24. Whipple, *Lights and Shadows*, 106.
25. Whipple, *Lights and Shadows*, 108.
26. Folwell, *A History of Minnesota*, 2:216–17.
27. Heard, *History*, 25–26.
28. Whipple, *Lights and Shadows*, 71.
29. Whipple, *Lights and Shadows*, 73.
30. Whipple, *Lights and Shadows*, 34–35.
31. Whipple, *Lights and Shadows*, 511.
32. Whipple, *Lights and Shadows*, 75.
33. Whipple, *Lights and Shadows*, 76.

Two: THE FIRST ATTACK

1. Henry Whipple, *Lights and Shadows of a Long Episcopate: Being Reminiscences and Recollections of the Right Reverend Henry Benjamin Whipple, D.D., LL.D.* (New York: Macmillan, 1912) 108.
2. Whipple, *Lights and Shadows*, 109.
3. Asa W. Daniels, "Reminiscences of Little Crow," *Collections of the Minnesota Historical Society*, vol. 12 (Saint Paul: Collections of the Minnesota Historical Society) 514–15.
4. Daniels, *Reminiscences*, 521.
5. Daniels, *Reminiscences*, 514–15.
6. Daniels, *Reminiscences*, 516.
7. Daniels, *Reminiscences*, 521.
8. Daniels, *Reminiscences*, 516; Gary Clayton Anderson, *Little Crow: Spokesman for the Sioux* (Saint Paul: Minnesota Historical Society, 1986) 44–45.
9. Henry Schoolcraft, *Historical and Statistical Information Respecting the History, Present and Prospects of the Indian Tribes of the United States*, Part I (Philadelphia: Lippincott and Grambo, 1851) 254.
10. James Lynd, *The History of the Dakota*, unpublished manuscript, 148, MHS manuscripts collections.

11. Kenneth Carley, *The Dakota War of 1862* (Saint Paul: Minnesota Historical Society, 1976) 10.
12. Gary Clayton Anderson and Alan Woolworth, editors, *Through Dakota Eyes: Narrative Accounts of the Minnesota Indian War of 1862* (Saint Paul: Minnesota Historical Society Press, 1988) 40.
13. Daniels, *Reminiscences*, 518; Anderson and Woolworth, *Through Dakota Eyes*, 40.
14. Anderson and Woolworth, *Through Dakota Eyes*, 39–42.
15. Samuel W. Pond, *Dakota Life in the Upper Midwest* (Saint Paul: Minnesota Historical Society, 1986) 9–10.
16. Anderson, *Little Crow*, 139–40.
17. Anderson, *Little Crow*, 141–42.
18. Lynd, *The History of the Dakota*, MHS manuscripts collections, 30.
19. Whipple, *Lights and Shadows*, 109.
20. George Tanner, *Fifty Years of Church Work in the Diocese of Minnesota, 1857–1907* (Saint Paul: Committee on Publication, 1909) 304.
21. Charles S. Bryant, *A History of the Great Massacre by the Sioux Indians in Minnesota* (Cincinnati: Rickey and Carroll, 1864) 93.
22. Ezmon W. Earle, "Reminiscences," 1907, MHS manuscripts collections.
23. Harry West, "A Lad's Version of Chief Little Crow," letter, July 29, 1933, MHS manuscripts collections.
24. G. G. Allanson, "Stirring Adventures of the Jos. R. Brown Family" (Sacred Heart, MN: Sacred Heart News, undated) unnumbered pages, MHS manuscripts collections.
25. Carley, *The Dakota War of 1862*, 16. Myrick's cruel statement is cited in most accounts of the Dakota War, as in Carley, *The Dakota War of 1862*, 6.
26. Whipple, *Lights and Shadows*, 111–12.

Three: LINCOLN AND THE INDIANS

1. Henry Whipple, *Lights and Shadows of a Long Episcopate: Being Reminiscences and Recollections of the Right Reverend Henry Benjamin Whipple, D.D., LL.D.* (New York: Macmillan, 1912) 20.
2. Whipple to Jonathan Whipple, letter, March 4, 1861; MHS manuscripts collections.
3. Michael Burlingame, *Abraham Lincoln: A Life*, vol. 2 (Baltimore: Johns Hopkins Univ. Press, 2008) 3–4, 32–34.
4. Whipple to Napoleon J. T. Dana, letter, February 23, 1861; MHS manuscripts collections.
5. Whipple to Jonathan Whipple, letter, March 4, 1861. MHS manuscripts collections.
6. Whipple, Sermon, first preached December 28, 1862, MHS manuscripts collections.
7. Whipple, Pastoral Letter to Diocese of Minnesota, April 17, 1861, MHS manuscripts collections.
8. Richard Moe, *The Last Full Measure: The Life and Death of the First Minnesota Volunteers* (New York: Avon, 1993) 7–8.
9. Whipple, *Lights and Shadows*, 96.

10. Whipple, *Lights and Shadows*, 136.
11. Burlingame, *Abraham Lincoln*, 1:573.
12. The Lincoln autobiographical essays may be found online, as at www .abrahamlincolnonline.org/lincoln/speeches/autobiog.htm.
13. Roy Basler, editor, *The Collected Works of Abraham Lincoln*, vol. 2 (New Brunswick, NJ: Rutgers Univ. Press, 1953) 217–18.
14. Burlingame, *Abraham Lincoln*, 1:1–2.
15. Robert Morgan, *Boone: A Biography* (Chapel Hill: Algonquin Books, 2007) 284; Michael Burlingame reports more than 100 white travelers killed on the road into Kentucky in 1784. Burlingame, *Abraham Lincoln*, 1:2.
16. Burlingame, *Abraham Lincoln*, 1:2.
17. Douglas Wilson and Rodney Davis, editors, *Herndon's Informants: Letters, Interviews and Statements about Abraham Lincoln* (Urbana and Chicago: University of Illinois, 1998) 95.
18. Wilson and Davis, *Herndon's Informants*, 36.
19. Wilson and Davis, *Herndon's Informants*, 96.
20. Wilson and Davis, *Herndon's Informants*, 220.
21. References to Hall and his short stories can be found at the website of their contemporary publisher, Kent State University Press: www.kentstate universitypress.com/2011/the-indian-hater-and-other-stories-by-james -hall/.
22. Burlingame, *Abraham Lincoln*, 1:23.
23. Carl Waldman, *The Atlas of the North American Indian* (New York: Facts on File, 1985) 117.
24. Andrew Clayton, *Frontier Indiana* (Bloomington: Univ. of Indiana, 1998) 261.
25. Ray A. Billington, "The Frontier in Illinois History," *Journal of the Illinois State Historical Society* 43 (Spring 1950): 30.
26. Joshua F. Speed, *Reminiscences of Abraham Lincoln* (Louisville, KY: John P. Morton, 1884) 25–26.
27. Black Hawk's words about the sale of land may be found in his autobiography and also quoted on the Wisconsin Historical Society's website, www.wisconsinhistory.org/diary/002693.asp. For information about Harrison's purchase of Indian lands, see Cecil Eby, *"That Disgraceful Affair:" The Black Hawk War* (New York: W. W. Norton, 1973) 46–47.
28. Eby, *"That Disgraceful Affair,"* 130–33.
29. Eby, *"That Disgraceful Affair,"* 248–55.
30. Burlingame, *Abraham Lincoln*, 1:70–71.
31. Wilson and Davis, *Herndon's Informants*, 362.
32. Wilson and Davis, *Herndon's Informants*, 362.
33. Eby, *"That Disgraceful Affair,"* 196.
34. Eby, *"That Disgraceful Affair,"* 145.
35. Wilson and Davis, *Herndon's Informants*, 372.
36. Wilson and Davis, *Herndon's Informants*, 372ff.
37. Wilson and Davis, *Herndon's Informants*, 363.
38. Wilson and Davis, *Herndon's Informants*, 372.
39. Wilson and Davis, *Herndon's Informants*, 372ff.

40. Wilson and Davis, *Herndon's Informants*, 390.
41. Wilson and Davis, *Herndon's Informants*, 18–19.
42. David Donald, *Lincoln* (New York: Simon & Schuster, 1995) 45; Burlingame, *Abraham Lincoln*, 1:69–70.

Four: THE DISPOSSESSED

1. Benjamin Scott and Robert Neslund, *The First Cathedral: An Episcopal Community for Mission* (Faribault, MN: Cathedral of Our Merciful Savior, 1987) 36.
2. Henry Whipple, *Lights and Shadows of a Long Episcopate: Being Reminiscences and Recollections of the Right Reverend Henry Benjamin Whipple, D.D., LL.D.* (New York: Macmillan, 1912) 122.
3. Whipple, *Lights and Shadows*, 122.
4. Whipple, *Lights and Shadows*, 122.
5. Alexander Ramsey to Edwin Stanton, Official Records, Civil War: Series One, vol. 13, August 25, 1862; Ramsey to Abraham Lincoln, Official Records, August 26, 1862.
6. Electa Currier to Henry Currier, letter, September 12, 1862, MHS manuscripts collections.
7. Whipple to Secretary of the Interior, letter, February 23, 1861, MHS manuscripts collections. Whipple to John Dix, letter, February 23, 1861, MHS manuscripts collections.
8. Whipple, *Lights and Shadows*, 122.
9. Betty Scandrett Oehler, *Bishop Whipple, Friend of the Indian*, 11–12, MHS manuscripts collections.
10. Whipple, *Lights and Shadows*, 122.
11. James Lynd, *The History of the Dakota*, unpublished manuscript, 19ff, MHS manuscripts collections.
12. William Lass, *The Treaty of Traverse des Sioux* (Saint Peter, MN: Nicollet County Historical Society, 2011) 20–21.
13. Lass, *Treaty of Traverse des Sioux*, 29.
14. Lass, *Treaty of Traverse des Sioux*, 41.
15. Lass, *Treaty of Traverse des Sioux*, 57–58.
16. James Goodhue, article in *Saint Paul Pioneer*, April 8, 1852, reprinted as "Territorial Daguerreotypes" in *Minnesota History* 29, no. 3 (September 1948): 202.
17. Bertha L. Heilbron, editor, *With Pen and Pencil on the Frontier in 1851: The Diary and Sketches of Frank Blackwell Mayer* (Saint Paul: Minnesota Historical Society, 1986) 125–26.
18. Heilbron, *With Pen and Pencil*, 149.
19. Gary Clayton Anderson, *Little Crow: Spokesman for the Sioux* (Saint Paul: Minnesota Historical Society, 1986) 142.
20. Kenneth Carley, *The Dakota War of 1862* (Saint Paul: Minnesota Historical Society, 1976) 27.
21. Carley, *The Dakota War*, 34.
22. Russell W. Fridley, "Charles E. Flandrau, Attorney at War," *Minnesota History* 38, no. 3 (September 1962): 117.

23. Fridley, "Charles E. Flandrau, Attorney at War," 122.
24. W. H. Hazzard, "Autobiographical Sketch of Sioux Uprising Experiences," MHS manuscripts collections.
25. Carley, *The Dakota War*, 37.
26. Hazzard, "Autobiographical Sketch."
27. Thomas Hughes, "Collected Statements of the Sioux Outbreak in Butternut Valley Township, Blue Earth County, Minn." undated, MHS manuscripts collections.
28. Carly, *The Dakota War*, 38.

Five: A "War of Extermination"
  1. Henry Whipple, *Lights and Shadows of a Long Episcopate: Being Reminiscences and Recollections of the Right Reverend Henry Benjamin Whipple, D.D. LL.D.* (New York: Macmillan, 1912) 142.
  2. Morton Wilkinson to Whipple, letter, May 8, 1862, MHS manuscripts collections.
  3. Whipple, *Lights and Shadows*, 50.
  4. Ezmon Earl, "Reminiscences," 1907; and E. M. Eastman, letter, June 18, 1923, both in MHS manuscripts collections.
  5. Gary Clayton Anderson, *Little Crow: Spokesman for the Sioux* (Saint Paul: Minnesota Historical Society, 1986) 139.
  6. John Nicolay to Lincoln, Official Records, Civil War, August 27, 1862; Lincoln to Ramsey, Official Records, Civil War, August 27, 1862.
  7. Kenneth Carley, *The Dakota War of 1862* (Saint Paul: Minnesota Historical Society, 1976) 40–44.
  8. Rebecca MacAlmond, diary, MHS manuscripts collections.
  9. Rebecca MacAlmond, diary, MHS manuscripts collections.
 10. Mary Anna Marston Hallock, letter, MHS manuscripts collections.
 11. Nicolay to Stanton, Official Records, Civil War, August 27, 1862.
 12. Marion Satterlee, Authentic List of the Victims of the Indian Massacre and War 1862 to 1865, January 15, 1919, MHS manuscripts collections.
 13. Whipple, *Lights and Shadows*, 136.
 14. John Pope to Stanton, Official Records, Civil War, September 23, 1862.
 15. Copies of Pope's General Order No. 7 may be found at Civil War sites online, as at "The Civil War Day by Day," associated with the Louis Round Wilson Special Collections Library at the University of North Carolina at Chapel Hill, http://blogs.lib.unc.edu/civilwar/index.php/page/59/ (see July 20, 1862).
 16. Pope to Henry Halleck, Official Records, Civil War, September 23, 1862.
 17. Charles S. Bryant, *A History of the Great Massacre by the Sioux Indians in Minnesota* (Cincinnati: Rickey and Carroll, 1864) 334–35.
 18. MacAlmond, diary, MHS manuscripts collections.
 19. Sally Wood, letters; "Eliza" to Laura Guigg Swett, letter, both in MHS manuscripts collections.
 20. Electa Currier, letter; Mary Crowell, letter, both MHS manuscripts collections.

21. Pope to Henry Sibley, Official Records, Civil War, September 28, 1862.
22. The quotation, included in his message to a special session of the state legislature may be found at the website www.usdakotawar.org maintained by the Minnesota Historical Society.
23. Ramsey to Whipple, letter, September 9, 1862, MHS manuscripts collections.
24. Carley, *The Dakota War of 1862*, 62–63.
25. Rosanna Sturgis, letter, MHS manuscripts collections.
26. Bryant, *A History of the Great Massacre*, 274.
27. Bryant, *A History of the Great Massacre*, 315.
28. Bryant, *A History of the Great Massacre*, 300–1.
29. Harriet E. Bishop McConkey, *Dakota War Whoop: Indian Massacres and War in Minnesota* (Chicago: Lakeside Press, 1965) 31–32.
30. Mary Anna Marston Hallock, letter, MHS manuscripts collections.
31. Bryant, *A History of the Great Massacre*, 338.
32. Bryant, *A History of the Great Massacre*, 339–40.
33. Mary Schwandt-Schmidt, "The Story of Mary Schwandt: Her Captivity During the Sioux 'Outbreak' 1862," MHS manuscripts collections accessed through University of California digital library, 474.

Six: WHIPPLE'S DAKOTA ALLIES AND THE WAR'S END

1. Henry Whipple, *Lights and Shadows of a Long Episcopate: Being Reminiscences and Recollections of the Right Reverend Henry Benjamin Whipple, D.D., LL.D.* (New York: Macmillan, 1912) 109.
2. Whipple, *Lights and Shadows*, 122–23.
3. Mary Schwandt-Schmidt, "The Story of Mary Schwandt: Her Captivity During the Sioux 'Outbreak' 1862," MHS manuscripts collections accessed through University of California digital library, 470–71.
4. Gary Clayton Anderson and Alan Woolrich, editors, *Through Dakota Eyes: Narrative Accounts of the Minnesota Indian War of 1862* (Saint Paul: Minnesota Historical Society, 1988) 142–43.
5. Margareta Holl Hahn, interview with Irene Persons, March 24, 1937. MHS manuscripts collections.
6. Nancy Winona McClure Huggan, letter to Gov. William R. Marshall, May 1894, MHS manuscripts collections.
7. Nancy Winona McClure Huggan, to Gov. William R. Marshall, May 1894.
8. Anderson and Woolworth, *Through Dakota Eyes*, 195–96.
9. Benjamin Scott and Robert Neslund, *The First Cathedral: An Episcopal Community for Mission* (Faribault, MN: Cathedral of Our Merciful Savior, 1987) 40–41.
10. Whipple, *Lights and Shadows*, 113.
11. Whipple, *Lights and Shadows*, 117–18.
12. Whipple, *Lights and Shadows*, 119–21.
13. Sarah F. Wakefield, *Six Weeks in Sioux Tepees: A Narrative of Indian Captivity*, (Norman: Univ. of Oklahoma, 1997) 84.
14. Wakefield, *Six Weeks in Sioux Tepees*, 55.

15. Wakefield, *Six Weeks in Sioux Tepees,* 61.
16. Wakefield, *Six Weeks in Sioux Tepees,* 64.

Seven: TO THE GATES OF MERCY
  1. Ramsey to Whipple, letter, September 9, 1862, MHS manuscripts collections.
  2. Samuel Chase to Lincoln, business card with written message, MHS manuscripts collections. The card—which is not dated—is included among MHS material pertaining to Whipple in December 1862. As there is no evidence the bishop was in Washington in that month, the card would appear to refer to the earlier visit and to have been misplaced in the later section.
  3. Whipple, letter, MHS manuscripts collections.
  4. Henry Whipple, *Lights and Shadows of a Long Episcopate: Being Reminiscences and Recollections of the Right Reverend Henry Benjamin Whipple, D.D., LL.D.* (New York: Macmillan, 1912) 66.
  5. Whipple, *Lights and Shadows,* 66.
  6. Whipple to John Dix, letter, February 23, 1861, MHS manuscripts collections.
  7. Whipple to Secretary of the Interior, letter, February 23, 1861, MHS manuscripts collections.
  8. Whipple to Secretary of the Interior, February 23, 1861.
  9. Whipple to R. M. Larned, letter, April 15, 1862, MHS manuscripts collections.
 10. Whipple to Lincoln, letter, March 6, 1862, MHS manuscripts collections.
 11. Michael Burlingame, *Abraham Lincoln: A Life,* vol. 2 (Baltimore: Johns Hopkins Univ. Press, 2008) 297–99; 335.
 12. Whipple to Lincoln, letter, March 6, MHS manuscripts collections.
 13. Whipple to Lincoln, letter, April 16, 1862, MHS manuscripts collections. In this letter, Whipple warned Lincoln that when whites undermined traditional Indian leadership and abused Indians generally, Indians would most likely respond with "retaliation."
 14. Whipple to Morton Wilkinson, letter, April 30, 1862; Whipple to Cyrus Aldrich, letter, April 30, 1862, both MHS manuscripts collections.
 15. Congressional Research Service, report, February 26, 2010, "American War and Military Operations Casualties: Lists and Statistics."
 16. Burlingame, *Abraham Lincoln,* 2:344–45.
 17. Greeley's appeal and Lincoln's reply are widely available online, the latter at such sites as www.abrahamlincolnonline.org/lincoln/speeches/greeley.htm.
 18. Greeley's appeal and Lincoln's reply are widely available online.
 19. Roy Basler, editor, *The Collected Works of Abraham Lincoln,* vol. 5 (New Brunswick, NJ: Rutgers Univ. Press, 1953) 403–4.
 20. Burlingame, *Abraham Lincoln,* 2:407–8.
 21. Basler, *Collected Works,* 5:344–46.
 22. Photographs and other illustrations of the White House at the time may be found on the Internet, at such sites as www.mrlincolnswhitehouse.org/index.asp.

23. Whipple, *Lights and Shadows*, 136–37.
24. Whipple, *Lights and Shadows*, 137.
25. Whipple, *Lights and Shadows*, 137.
26. Whipple, *Lights and Shadows*, 137–38.
27. Whipple to Ezekiel Gear, letter, November 5, 1862, MHS manuscripts collections.
28. Whipple to Gear, MHS manuscripts collections; Whipple, *Lights and Shadows*, 96.
29. Richard Moe, *The Last Full Measure: The Life and Death of the First Minnesota Volunteers* (New York: Avon, 1993) 190.
30. Whipple to Gear, MHS manuscripts collections.
31. Whipple, *Lights and Shadows*, 98–99.

Eight: MAINTAINING THE PRESSURE

1. "The Episcopal Convention," *New York Times*, October 9, 1862.
2. Henry Whipple, *Lights and Shadows of a Long Episcopate: Being Reminiscences and Recollections of the Right Reverend Henry Benjamin Whipple, D.D., LL.D.* (New York: Macmillan, 1912) 138.
3. Whipple, *Lights and Shadows*, 138.
4. William Seward to Lincoln, letter, October 25, 1862, Abraham Lincoln Papers in the Library of Congress, Series One.
5. Whipple, *Lights and Shadows*, 140.
6. "Sermon by Bishop Whipple, of Minnesota," *New York Times*, October 6, 1862.
7. Isaac Heard, *The History of the Sioux War* (New York: Harper & Brothers, 1864) 251.
8. Kenneth Carley, *The Dakota War of 1862* (Saint Paul: Minnesota Historical Society, 1976) 64–67.
9. Heard, *History*, 251.
10. Pope to Halleck, Official Records, Civil War, October 9, 1862.
11. Heard, *History*, 254.
12. Heard, *History*, 254.
13. Heard, *History*, 266.
14. Heard, *History*, 267.
15. Sibley to Pope, Official Records, Civil War, October 21, 1862.
16. Carley, *The Dakota War of 1862*, 69.
17. Heard, *History*, 268.
18. Ramsey to Lincoln, Official Records, Civil War, November 10, 1862.
19. Ramsey to Lincoln, Official Records, Civil War, November 10, 1862.
20. Carley, *The Dakota War of 1862*, 70.
21. Lincoln to Pope, Official Records, Civil War, November 10, 1862.
22. Pope to Lincoln, Official Records, Civil War, November 11, 1862.
23. Pope to Lincoln, Official Records, Civil War, November 11, 1862.
24. Pope to Lincoln, Official Records, Civil War, November 11, 1862.
25. Pope to Lincoln, Official Records, Civil War, November 11, 1862.
26. Whipple to Elizabeth Whipple, letter, October 24, 1862, MHS manuscripts collections.

27. Whipple to Elizabeth Whipple, letter, October 24, 1862, MHS manuscripts collections.
28. William Watts Folwell, *A History of Minnesota*, vol. 2 (Saint Paul: Minnesota Historical Society, 1961) 203.
29. Folwell, *A History of Minnesota*, 2:203.
30. David Nichols, "The Other Civil War: Lincoln and the Indians," *Minnesota History* 44, no. 1 (Spring 1974): 9.
31. Jane L. Williamson to the Rev. Stephen R. Riggs, letter, November 14, 1862, Abraham Lincoln Papers.
32. Riggs to Lincoln, November 17, 1862, letter, Abraham Lincoln Papers.
33. Riggs to Lincoln, November 17, 1862, letter, Abraham Lincoln Papers.
34. William P. Dole to Caleb B. Smith, letter, November 10, 1862, Abraham Lincoln Papers.
35. Whipple to Gear, letter, November 5, 1862, MHS manuscripts collections.
36. Whipple to Henry Rice, letter, November 12, 1862, MHS manuscripts collections.
37. Rice to Whipple, letter, November 19, 1862, MHS manuscripts collections.
38. Rice to Lincoln, letter, November 20, 1862, Abraham Lincoln Papers.

Nine: JUDGMENT AND REASON

1. Lincoln's Second Message to Congress may be found on the web, at such sites as the University of California's American Presidency Project, www.presidency.ucsb.edu/ws/?pid=29503.
2. Lincoln's Second Message to Congress.
3. Whipple to Lincoln, letter, December 4, 1862, MHS manuscripts collections.
4. Roy Basler, editor, *The Collected Works of Abraham Lincoln*, vol. 5 (New Brunswick, NJ: Rutgers Univ. Press, 1953) 537–38; Joseph Holt to Lincoln, letter, December 1, 1862, Abraham Lincoln Papers.
5. Henry Whipple, "The Duty of Citizens Concerning the Indian Massacre," *Saint Paul Pioneer,* December 3, 1862, reprinted in Whipple's *Lights and Shadows of a Long Episcopate: Being Reminiscences and Recollections of the Right Reverend Henry Benjamin Whipple, D.D., LL.D.* (New York: Macmillan, 1912) 123–30.
6. Tim Post, "A Woman of Contradiction," Minnesota Public Radio, September 26, 2002, available at http://news.minnesota.publicradio.org/features/200209/23_steilm_1862-m/swisshelm.shtml.
7. Sylvia D. Hoffert, "Gender and Vigilantism on the Minnesota Frontier: Jane Grey Swissholm and the U. S. Dakota Conflict of 1862," *Western Historical Quarterly* (Autumn 1998): 349.
8. Sylvia Hoffert, "Gender and Vigilantism," 357.
9. Winfred Harbison, "President Lincoln and the Faribault Fire-Eater," *Minnesota History* 20, no. 3 (September 1939): 271.
10. *Central Republican*, editorials, Faribault, MN, August 27, September 3, and October 15, 1862.
11. Whipple to Rice, letter, November 12, 1862, MHS manuscripts collections.

12. Whipple, "The Duty of Citizens," *Saint Paul Pioneer*, reprinted in Whipple's *Lights and Shadows*.
13. Whipple, undated letter to the editor of the *Saint Paul Pioneer*, MHS manuscripts collections.
14. Basler, *Collected Works*, 5:542–43.
15. Henry Sibley to Abraham Lincoln, letter, December 15, 1862, Abraham Lincoln Papers at the Library of Congress.
16. Frank Gauthier to Sibley, letter, December 15, 1862, MHS manuscripts collections.
17. Charles McColley, "An Indian Pentecost," undated, MHS manuscripts collections.
18. Kenneth Carley, *The Dakota War of 1862* (Saint Paul: Minnesota Historical Society, 1976) 76.
19. Whipple, *Lights and Shadows*, 515.
20. Whipple, *Lights and Shadows*, 516.
21. Charles McColley, "An Indian Pentecost," undated, MHS manuscripts collections.
22. Julius Owens, letter, MHS manuscripts collections.
23. Marcia Doughty Pike, interview, November 17, 1940, *The Sunday Oregonian*, MHS manuscripts collections.
24. John Meagher, letter, December 26, 1887, MHS manuscripts collections.
25. *The London Times* correspondent Francis Charles Lawley's "Account of the Battle of Fredericksburg" is quoted in Margaret E. Wagner, Gary W. Gallagher, and Paul Finkelman, editors, *Library of Congress Civil War Desk Reference* (New York: Simon & Schuster, 2002) 273.
26. Richard Moe, *The Last Full Measure: The Life and Death of the First Minnesota Volunteers* (New York: Avon, 1993) 231.
27. Whipple, sermon, December 28, 1862, MHS manuscripts collections.
28. Whipple, sermon, December 28, 1862, MHS manuscripts collections.
29. Whipple, sermon, December 28, 1862, MHS manuscripts collections.
30. William Marshall to Whipple, letter, December 19, 1862, MHS manuscripts collections.

Ten: EXILE AND COMMUNITY

1. Charles McColley, "An Indian Pentecost," undated reminiscence, MHS manuscripts collections.
2. McColley, "An Indian Pentecost."
3. Jennifer Graber, "Mighty Upheaval on the Minnesota Frontier: Violence, War, and Death in Dakota and Missionary Christianity," *Church History* 80, no. 1 (March 2011): 100; and Kenneth Carley, *The Dakota War of 1862* (Saint Paul: Minnesota Historical Society, 1976) 70.
4. Henry Whipple, *Lights and Shadows of a Long Episcopate: Being Reminiscences and Recollections of the Right Reverend Henry Benjamin Whipple, D.D., LL.D.* (New York: Macmillan, 1912) 133.
5. Jennifer Graber, "Mighty Upheaval on the Minnesota Frontier," 104.
6. Whipple, *Lights and Shadows*, 160.

7. William Lass, "The Removal from Minnesota of the Sioux and Winnebago Indians," *Minnesota History* 38, no. 4 (December 1963): 359.

8. Lass, "The Removal from Minnesota," 364.

9. Whipple, *Lights and Shadows*, 133–35.

10. Benjamin Scott and Robert Neslund, *The First Cathedral: An Episcopal Community for Mission* (Faribault, MN: Cathedral of Our Merciful Savior, 1987) 37–39.

11. Carley, *The Dakota War of 1862*, 91.

12. Gary Clayton Anderson, *Little Crow: Spokesman for the Sioux* (Saint Paul: Minnesota Historical Society, 1986) 178; and Carley, *The Dakota War of 1862*, 86.

13. Whipple, *Lights and Shadows*, 143–44.

14. Whipple, *Lights and Shadows*, 144.

15. Whipple, *Lights and Shadows*, 535–46.

16. Whipple, *Lights and Shadows*, 144.

17. Whipple, *Lights and Shadows*, 238–39.

18. Whipple, *Lights and Shadows*, 149.

Bibliography

Note: "MHS" refers to the Minnesota Historical Society.

DOCUMENTS

Whipple collection, Minnesota Historical Society.

Manuscripts collections, Minnesota Historical Society.

Manuscripts collections, Historical Association of South Jefferson, Adams, NY.

Abraham Lincoln Papers, Library of Congress.

Central Republican. Faribault, MN. August–October 1862.

Lynd, James. *The History of the Dakota*. Unpublished manuscript. MHS manuscripts collections.

New York Times, October 1862.

Official Records, Civil War, Series One, Vol. XIII.

Oehler, Betty Scandrett. "Bishop Whipple, Friend of the Indian." MHS manuscripts collections.

Schwandt-Schmidt, Mary. "The Story of Mary Schwandt: Her Captivity During the Sioux 'Outbreak' 1862." MHS manuscripts collections.

Thomas, Margaret Luce. "Enmegahbowh: Native and Christian." Paper for class, Pacific School of Religion. December 16, 1994. http://archive .episcopalchurch.org/documents/NAM_Enmegahbowh_Native_and_ Christian.pdf.

U.S. Department of the Interior. "Ratified Treaty No. 108, Documents Relating to the Negotiation of the Treaty of June 19, 1858, with the Mdwakantons and Wahpekuta Sioux Indians."

ARTICLES

Billington, Ray A. "The Frontier in Illinois History." *Journal of the Illinois State Historical Society* 43 (Spring 1950).

Congressional Research Service, report, February 26, 2010, "American War and Military Operations Casualties: Lists and Statistics."

Daniels, Asa. "Reminiscences of Little Crow." *Collections of the Minnesota Historical Society* 12.

Fridley, Russell. "Charles E. Flandrau, Attorney at War." *Minnesota History* 38, no. 3 (September 1962).

Goodhue, James. Article in *Saint Paul Pioneer*, April 8, 1852, reprinted as "Territorial Daguerreotypes" in *Minnesota History* 29, no. 3 (September 1948).

Graber, Jennifer. "Mighty Upheaval on the Minnesota Frontier: Violence, War, and Death in Dakota and Missionary Christianity." *Church History* 80, no. 1 (March 2011).

Harbison, Winfred. "President Lincoln and the Faribault Fire-Eater." *Minnesota History* 20, no. 3 (September 1939).

Lass, William. "The Removal from Minnesota of the Sioux and Winnebago Indians." *Minnesota History* 38, no. 4 (December 1963).

Nichols, David. "The Other Civil War: Lincoln and the Indians." *Minnesota History* 44, no. 1 (Spring 1974).

Post, Tim. "A Woman of Contradiction." Minnesota Public Radio, September 26, 2002,

BOOKS

Anderson, Gary Clayton. *Little Crow: Spokesman for the Sioux*. Saint Paul: Minnesota Historical Society, 1986.

Anderson, Gary Clayton and Alan Woolrich, eds., *Through Dakota Eyes: Narrative Accounts of the Minnesota Indian War of 1862*. Saint Paul: Minnesota Historical Society Press, 1988.

Basler, Roy, ed., *The Collected Works of Abraham Lincoln*. Vols. 2 and 5. New Brunswick, NJ: Rutgers Univ. Press, 1953.

Beard, Augustus Field. *A History of the American Missionary Association*. Boston: Pilgrim Press, 1910.

Berleth, Richard. *Bloody Mohawk: The French and Indian War and American Revolution on New York's Frontier*. Hensonville, NY: Black Dome, 2009.

Bryant, Charles. *A History of the Great Massacre by the Sioux Indians in Minnesota*. Cincinnati: Rickey and Carroll, 1864.

Burlingame, Michael. *Abraham Lincoln: A Life*. Vols. 1 and 2. Baltimore: Johns Hopkins University Press, 2008.

Carley, Kenneth. *The Dakota War of 1862*. Saint Paul: Minnesota Historical Society, 1976.

Child, Hamilton. *Geographic Gazetteer of Jefferson County*. Syracuse: Syracuse Journal, 1890.

Donald, David. *Lincoln*. New York: Simon & Schuster, 1995.

Eby, Cecil. *"That Disgraceful Affair:" The Black Hawk War*. New York: W.W. Norton, 1973.

Folwell, William Watts. *A History of Minnesota*. Vol. 2. Saint Paul: Minnesota Historical Society, 1924.

Heard, Isaac. *The History of the Sioux War*. New York: Harper & Brothers, 1864.

Heilbron, Bertha L., ed. *With Pen and Pencil on the Frontier in 1851: The Diary and Sketches of Frank Blackwell Mayer*. Saint Paul: Minnesota Historical Society, 1986.

Hubbard, Lucian and Return Holcome. *Minnesota in Three Centuries.* Vol. 3. Mankato, MN: Publishing Society of Minnesota, 1908.

Lass, William. *The Treaty of Traverse des Sioux.* Saint Peter, MN: Nicollet County Historical Society, 2011.

McConkey, Harriet E. Bishop. *Dakota War Whoop: Indian Massacres and War in Minnesota.* Chicago: Lakeside Press, 1965.

Moe, Richard. *The Last Full Measure: The Life and Death of the First Minnesota Volunteers.* New York: Avon, 1993.

Morgan, Robert. *Boone: A Biography.* Chapel Hill: Algonquin Books, 2007.

Nichols, David. *Lincoln and the Indians: Civil War Policy and Politics.* Columbia: Univ. of Missouri, 1978.

O'Toole, Fintan. *White Savage: William Johnson and the Invention of America.* New York: Farrar, Straus and Giroux, 2005.

Pond, Samuel W. *Dakota Life in the Upper Midwest.* Saint Paul: Minnesota Historical Society, 1986.

Prucha, Francis Paul. *The Great Father: The United States Government and the American Indians.* Vol. 1. Lincoln: Univ. of Nebraska, 1984.

Robinson, Doane. *A History of the Dakota or Sioux Indians.* Minneapolis: Ross & Haines, 1967.

Schoolcraft, Henry. *Historical and Statistical Information Respecting the History, Present and Prospects of the Indian Tribes of the United States.* Part I. Philadelphia: Lippincott and Grambo, 1851.

Scott, Benjamin and Robert Neslund. *The First Cathredral: An Episcopal Community for Mission.* Faribault, MN: Cathedral of Our Merciful Savior, 1987.

Shippee, Lester, ed. *Bishop Whipple's Southern Diary 1843–1844.* New York: Da Capo, 1968.

Speed, Joshua. *Reminiscences of Abraham Lincoln.* Louisville, KY: John P. Morton, 1884.

Tanner, George, *Fifty Years of Church Work in the Diocese of Minnesota, 1857–1907.* Saint Paul: Committee on Publication, 1909.

Thoreau, Henry David. *Letters to Various Persons.* Boston: James R. Osgood, 1877.

Waldman, Carl. *The Atlas of the North American Indian.* New York: Facts on File, 1985.

Whipple, Henry. *Lights and Shadows of a Long Episcopate: Being Reminiscences and Recollections of the Right Reverend Henry Benjamin Whipple, D.D., LL.D.* New York: Macmillan, 1912.

Wilson, Douglas and Rodney Davis, eds. *Herndon's Informants: Letters, Interviews and Statements about Abraham Lincoln.* Urbana and Chicago: University of Illinois, 1998.

Further Reading

Anyone wishing to gain greater knowledge of Bishop Whipple's life needs to read his autobiography, *Lights and Shadows of a Long Episcopate: Being the Reminiscences and Recollections of the Right Reverend Henry Benjamin Whipple, Bishop of Minnesota*. Whipple wrote this memoir in the final decade of his life and produced a work more anecdotal than a conventional narrative. The book may be of greater value for that, along with its inclusion of important letters Whipple wrote and received, public appeals he authored and the testimony of Indians he befriended in Minnesota. Although the most useful book about the man himself, Whipple wrote another, shorter autobiographical work, a diary he kept during the several months he toured the South as a twenty-one-year-old in 1843–44. *Bishop Whipple's Southern Diary* did not see publication until nearly a century later. It contains observations of a very young man on African American slavery and the white families who benefited from it. Outside of a brief meditation on the treachery involved in the U.S. Government's capture of the Seminole chief Osceola, Whipple gives little indication of the concern for Native American welfare that would so drive him later.

In 2008, Afton Historical Society Press published a generously illustrated, large-format biography of Whipple. *And the Wilderness Shall Blossom: Henry Benjamin Whipple, Churchman, Educator, Advocate for the Indians*, provides the linear narrative of Whipple's life largely absent from *Lights and Shadows*. Anne B. Allen also fleshes out various Whipple anecdotes, not least his fondness for his horse Bashaw.

Appropriately, the bishop is accorded varying degrees of recognition in general histories written about the Dakota War. Kenneth Carley's *The Dakota War of 1862: Minnesota's Other Civil War*, long a basic text of the conflict, describes Whipple's as the "[o]nly one really effective voice from Minnesota" arguing against the military's plan to hang all 303 Dakotas. Duane Schultz, in *Over the Earth I Come: The Great Sioux Uprising of 1862*, gives Whipple a brief, respectful nod. In *38 Nooses: Lincoln, Little Crow and the Beginning of the Frontier's*

End, Scott W. Berg offers a nicely written and concise account of Whipple's visit to Washington and his meeting with Lincoln.

In his book on the Lincoln administration's Indian policies, *Lincoln and the Indians: Civil War Politics and Policies*, David Nichols affords Whipple credit for his work, but argues the bishop eventually became disappointed in his hopes Lincoln would reform the Indian office.

Not all writing about Whipple has been positive. Martin Zanger, in an essay in *Churchmen and the Western Indians, 1820 to 1920*, praises Whipple's dedication to justice for the Indians, but—reviewing the bishop's work with the Ojibwe—faults him for the damage done to their culture by his (and others') missionary efforts. In 2005, Andrew Brake came to Whipple's measured defense, in *Man in the Middle: The Reform and Influence of Henry Benjamin Whipple, the First Episcopal Bishop of Minnesota*, by arguing that Whipple's work did not stem from a blind faith in "civilization," but from determination to secure justice for Native Americans.

One can reasonably expect more appraisals of Whipple: the man was simply too interesting, too determined in his work, too dedicated to justice to be forgotten in history.

$Index$